SEW THE PERFECT BAG

25 GREAT PROJECTS FROM *SEW NEWS*

Martingale & Company
20205 144th Ave. NE
Woodinville, WA 98072-8478 USA
www.martingale-pub.com

SewNews, ISSN 0273-8120, is published bimonthly by Creative Crafts Group, LLC, 741 Corporate Circle, Suite A, Golden, CO 80401, www.sewnews.com

Printed in China

15 14 13 12 11 10   8 7 6 5 4 3 2 1

Library of Congress Cataloging-in-Publication Data is available upon request.

ISBN: 978-1-60468-024-9

CREDITS

President & CEO: Tom Wierzbicki
Editor in Chief: Mary V. Green
Managing Editor: Tina Cook
Design Director: Stan Green
Consulting Editor: Laurie Baker
Copy Editor: Melissa Bryan
Production Manager: Regina Girard
Illustrator: Laurel Strand
Cover & Text Designer: Stan Green
Photographers: Joe Hancock Photography, Brent Kane, Brent Ward Photography

MISSION STATEMENT

Dedicated to providing quality products and service to inspire creativity.

CONTENTS

page 44

page 87

page 59

page 5

page 20

page 51

INTRODUCTION
WHO DOESN'T LOVE A NEW BAG?

You may call it a purse, pocketbook, handbag, clutch, backpack or satchel, but we're calling it a bag. A bag is a sewer's best friend. It doesn't need to be perfect. It doesn't need to fit. It doesn't need to match. All it needs to do is look cute and hold your belongings—whether you're toting a lipstick and wallet or a week's worth of paperwork, an umbrella and extra gym clothes.

The first sewing project I ever made was a purse. I didn't use a pattern and tried to patch together a few fabric squares to construct a simple rectangular purse with a flap and button closure. To my dismay, I didn't know a thing about seam allowances and the purse quickly came apart before it was even finished. I've since learned a lot about purse construction and have made more bags than I can count. A bag is a great project, whether you're a beginning, intermediate or advanced sewer, because you can use funky fabrics and experiment with shapes and sizes. For very little investment (some bags in this book require less than a yard of fabric) and very little time (some can be made in an hour or less), you can complete a new bag that's unlike anything you could buy in a store.

Many of the bags in this book don't require an actual pattern. They're made with a series of rectangles or squares that are easy to adapt to your style. Once you finish one pattern-free bag, you'll see just how easy it is to create your own bag patterns and add pockets, snaps, zippers and embellishments to your heart's content. Valuable tips and tricks from the bag designers will help you along the way. And illustrated steps will take the guesswork out of the construction process.

There's a bag for every season and every reason, from book bags to evening bags to diaper bags. Be prepared to need another closet!

Happy Sewing,
Ellen March
Sew News Editor

FRENCH MARKET TOTE

Designed by Kaari Meng

HEAD TO THE FARMER'S MARKET
in style with this chic patchwork tote.
It's a great project for using up those
pretty leftover scraps that you just
can't seem to throw out.

Finished size: 15" x 17" (excluding straps)

SUPPLIES

Yardages are based on 44"/45"-wide fabric.

• ¾ yard total of assorted coordinating ligh-to-medium weight fabric scraps for bag exterior

• ¾ yard of linen for lining

• Matching all-purpose thread

• Rotary cutter and mat (optional)

• Tube turner or bodkin (optional)

tip

Use a rotary cutter and mat to cut super-straight and even edges.

CUTTING

From the assorted fabric scraps, cut a variety of rectangles and squares for piecing together. The final finished front should be 16" x 17½". For the featured tote pieces, refer to the cutting diagram (fig. A). Cut identical pieces or a different shape assortment totaling 16" x 17½" for the tote back. From one of the selected fabrics, cut two 2" x 22" strips for the straps.

From the linen, cut two 16" x 17½" rectangles for the lining.

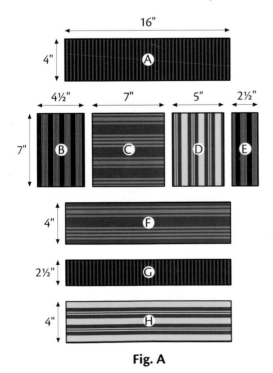

Fig. A

CONSTRUCTING THE TOTE

Sew with right sides together and a ½" seam allowance unless otherwise noted.

1. For the featured tote, sew pieces B and C together along one 7" edge. Repeat to stitch piece D to piece C. Then stitch piece E to piece D to create a 7" x 16" center panel. Press open all seams (fig. B).

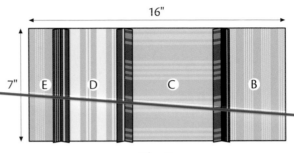

Fig. B

2. Topstitch around each piece perimeter, about ⅛" from the edge (fig. C).

Fig. C

3. Stitch piece A to the center panel. Press open the seam and topstitch around the piece A perimeter. Repeat to attach and topstitch pieces F, G and H to complete the tote front (fig. D). Piece and topstitch the tote back, accordingly.

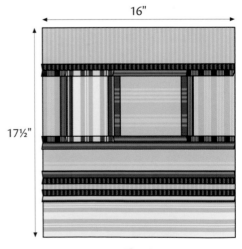

Fig. D

4. To make the straps, fold one 2" x 22" strip in half lengthwise; press. Stitch the long edge. Use a tube turner or bodkin to turn the strap right side out. Press flat. Edgestitch both long edges. Repeat to create the second strap.

5. Position the short ends of one strap on the tote front right side upper edge, about 4" from each side edge. Baste the strap short ends in place (fig. E). Repeat to baste the other strap to the tote back.

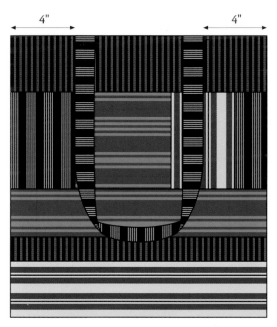

Fig. E

6. Position the tote front and back right sides together. Stitch the side seams, leaving the lower edge open. Press open the seams. Repeat with the lining pieces.

7. Position the tote outer layer inside the lining with right sides together, making sure the straps stay inside the two layers. Stitch around the tote upper edge. Turn the tote outer layer to the right side through the open lower edge.

8. Turn the tote inside out. Stitch the lower edge through all the fabric layers. Finish the seam with a serger or zigzag stitch if desired.

9. Turn the tote right side out. Topstitch around the upper edge, about ⅜" from the edge. Topstitch again, about ¹⁄₁₆" from the upper edge (fig. F).

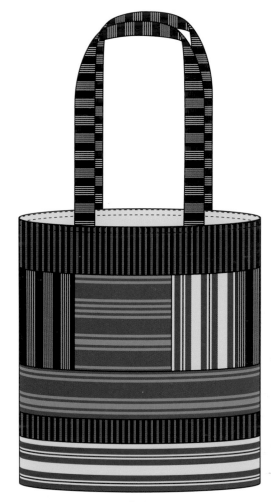

Fig. F

A linen lining is both sturdy and lightweight.

TECHNO TOTE

Designed by Shannon Dennis

YOUR LAPTOP WILL BE HEADED FOR THE LAP OF LUXURY when tucked away in this padded and embellished carrying case.

Finished tote size: 21¾" x 13¾" x 1¾" (excluding flap and strap)

SUPPLIES

- ½ yard of 54"-wide solid-color wool for bag exterior
- ¾ yard of 45"-wide print fabric for bag exterior
- Scraps of silk dupioni for embellishments
- Yarn remnants
- ½ yard of fusible fleece
- Thread: all-purpose, gold metallic
- Rotary-cutting tools
- Needle-punching machine or hand-felting tools

CUTTING

From the wool, cut one 15" x 23" rectangle for the body and one 14" x 15½" rectangle for the flap.

From the print fabric, cut four 3" x 15" rectangles for the sides, one 6" x 44" rectangle for the strap, one 15" x 23" rectangle for the bag lining and one 14" x 15½" rectangle for the flap lining.

From the fusible fleece, cut one 15" x 23" rectangle for the body, one 15" x 16½" rectangle for the flap and two 3" x 15" rectangles for the sides.

CONSTRUCTING THE TOTE

Sew with right sides together and a ⅝" seam allowance unless otherwise noted.

1. Use a steam iron to fuse the fusible fleece to the wrong side of the corresponding body, side and flap pieces (not the lining pieces).

2. To embellish the bag flap, arrange silk and yarn pieces on the flap right side. Use a needle-punching machine or hand-felting tools to felt the silk and yarn into the wool. Add decorative stitching as desired (see photo and "Personalizing Your Bag" on page 10 for placement and ideas).

3. Trim any flap embellishments and the excess fleece even with the flap edges. Place the flap and flap lining pieces together. Designate one long edge as the upper edge. Stitch around the flap sides and lower edge leaving the upper edge open. Clip the corners and turn the flap right side out; press. Topstitch ¼" from the side and lower edges.

4. With the upper edges aligned, place one fused side piece along one body side edge. Stitch, stopping ⅝" from the side piece lower corner (fig. A). Keep the needle in the fabric.

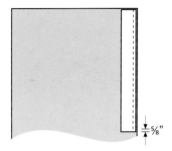

Fig. A

5. Clip a scant ½" into the body piece where the stitching ended (fig. B). This allows the body fabric to pivot more easily at the corner.

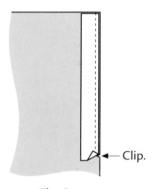

← Clip.

Fig. B

6. Pivot the body fabric to align the short edge of the side piece with the body raw edge; stitch to within ⅝" of the next corner (fig. C).

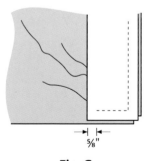

⅝"

Fig. C

7. Clip and pivot again to stitch the second side piece long edge to the body. Repeat to attach the second fused side piece to the body.

8. Repeat to attach the lining side pieces to the lining body.

9. Wrong sides together, fold the 6"-wide strap in half lengthwise. Press the fold. Unfold the strap and fold both long edges toward the center crease; press. Refold the strap, encasing the raw edges. Topstitch ¼" from each long edge.

10. Center the flap unsewn edge along the body upper edge with right sides together; baste. Pin the strap ends on the body back approximately 2" in from each side and at least 1" below where the flap attaches to the bag. Adjust the strap position so it fits comfortably. Tuck under each strap raw end ½". Secure the strap to the bag by stitching a box shape on each end (fig. D).

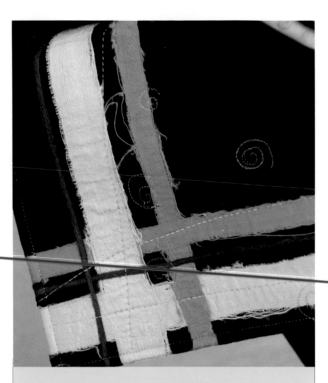

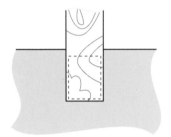

Fig. D

11. Turn the lining inside out and pin it to the body; align all the seams and raw edges. Stitch, leaving a 5" opening along one edge for turning.

12. Turn the bag right side out; press. Slipstitch the opening closed.

PERSONALIZING YOUR BAG

Designer Shannon Dennis used torn strips of silk dupioni to embellish her bag, but you could instead stitch strips of cotton to your version.

If a tidy look sounds appealing, consider turning under the edges of your fabric embellishments before stitching them down. If you're looking for a little excitement, consider adding a sprinkling of bright beads.

BABY ON BOARD

Designed by Ellen March

WHETHER YOU HAVE ONE CHILD OR MANY, this bag will hold everything they might need on an outing—it's even big enough to carry some of *your* necessities!

This diaper bag has an attached vinyl pad for quick-and-sanitary changing. The side pockets each hold two full-size baby bottles and the zippered pocket corrals small items. Choose either a messenger-style strap or backpack straps—or both; they're removable and easily change to fit your mood. Lengthen the backpack straps to hook the bag around stroller handles.

Finished bag size: 15¾" x 14" x 6" (excluding straps)

SUPPLIES

Yardages are based on 44"/45"-wide fabric unless otherwise noted.

- 3 yards of fashion fabric for bag exterior
- 2¾ yards of fabric for lining
- ½ yard of 54"-wide flannel-backed vinyl (such as Baby Dry)
- 1¾ yards of 22"-wide stiff interfacing (such as Timtex)
- ½ yard of 90"-wide high-loft batting
- 16"-long matching zipper
- 2" x 13" strip of hook-and-loop tape
- Two ¾" x 7" elastic strips
- D-rings: two 1¼" wide, four 2" wide
- Six 2"-wide metal snap hooks
- Three 2"-wide metal single bars
- Removable fabric marker
- Matching thread
- Temporary spray adhesive (optional)

CUTTING

Read all the dimensions carefully prior to cutting and label each piece after cutting. To label each piece, use a removable fabric marker on the fabric wrong side or attach a sticky note to the fabric. The cutting dimensions include ½" seam allowances.

From the fashion fabric, cut five 15" x 16¾" rectangles for the body, one 9½" x 16¾" rectangle for the flap, two 3½" x 16¾" rectangles for the upper flap, two 7¾" x 16¾" rectangles for the lower flap, one 7" x 16¾" rectangle for the base, and two 7" x 15" rectangles for the sides. Also cut two 8½" x 12" rectangles for the pocket, one 4" x 72" rectangle for the messenger strap, four 4" squares for the tab, two 2¼" x 3½" rectangles for the backpack tab, two 1¼" squares for the zipper tabs, and two 2" x 18" strips for the tie.

From the lining fabric, cut two 15" x 16¾" rectangles for the body, three 9½" x 16¾" rectangles for the flap, one 7" x 16¾" rectangle for the base, and two 7" x 15" rectangles for the side. Also cut two 8½" x 12" rectangles for the pocket, two 1¼" squares for the zipper tabs, and two 4" x 44" rectangles for the backpack strap.

From the stiff interfacing, cut two 14" x 15¾" rectangles for the body, one 6" x 15¾" rectangle for the base, and two 6" x 14" rectangles for the side.

From the batting, cut one 14" x 15¾" rectangle and one 15½" x 42" rectangle.

From the vinyl, cut one 16¾" x 43½" rectangle.

CONSTRUCTING THE CHANGING PAD

Sew with right sides together and a ½" seam allowance unless otherwise noted.

1. Position the loop side of the hook-and-loop tape 1" from the long upper edge and 2" from either short edge of one fabric body; pin. Satin stitch the loop-piece perimeter. Tie off the thread tails on the fabric wrong side, and press from the wrong side.

2. Right sides together, stitch three fabric body pieces together along the long edges, placing the section with the loop piece in the center (fig. A). Press open the seams.

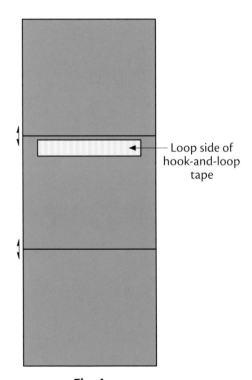

Loop side of hook-and-loop tape

Fig. A

3. Center the large batting rectangle over the pieced section wrong side. Secure the batting with temporary spray adhesive or pin baste the perimeter.

4. Place the vinyl rectangle right side up on a flat work surface. Right sides together, position the batting-lined fabric over the vinyl, aligning the corners and edges. Stitch the long edges and one short edge; leave open the short end closest to the hook-and-loop tape (fig. B).

5. Turn the changing pad right side out with the batting between the layers. Press from the fabric side, and then topstitch the pad perimeter. Stitch in the ditch along each fabric seam, beginning at the seam center and stitching outward to the topstitched seam. Press from the fabric side. Set aside the pad.

CONSTRUCTING THE FLAP

1. Unzip the zipper halfway. Abut the zipper teeth and pin the zipper tape shut at the zipper-pull end. Mark a line across the pinned end ½" from the edge. Right sides together, align the fabric-zipper-tab edge with the mark; pin (fig. C). Flip over the zipper and repeat to pin the lining-zipper-tab edge to the zipper wrong side. Stitch, carefully maneuvering over the zipper teeth stops.

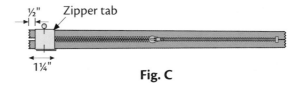

Fig. C

2. Fold the tabs back so wrong sides are facing and the zipper end is sandwiched between each fabric. Topstitch close to the seam. Repeat to stitch the remaining zipper tab to the opposite zipper end.

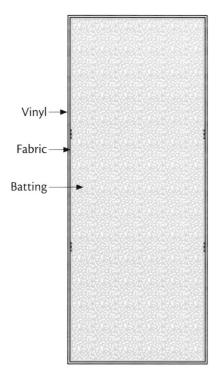

Vinyl →
Fabric →
Batting →

Fig. B
Layer batting-lined fabric over vinyl;
stitch long edges and one short edge.
Stitch body pieces together.

3. Right sides together, align one upper-flap long edge with the zipper upper edge (with the zipper stop to the right); pin. Flip over the zipper and align the remaining upper-flap edge with the zipper upper edge; pin. Stitch, using a zipper foot to stitch as close to the zipper teeth as possible. Fold each fabric back so wrong sides are facing; topstitch close to the seam. Repeat to stitch the lower-flap pieces to the zipper lower edge.

4. Right sides together, pin one lining flap to the zipper flap, aligning the corners and edges. Then pin another lining flap over the layers, with the lining wrong sides facing. Stitch the lower edge (farthest from the zipper) and short edges. Trim the seam allowances to ¼" and clip the corners. Turn right side out, press, and then topstitch.

5. Place the remaining lining flap right side up on a flat surface. Align the wrong side of the unfinished zipper flap

upper edge with one lining-flap long edge. Right sides together, place the fabric flap over the zipper flap. Stitch the upper edges and short ends, encasing the zipper-flap raw edge and keeping the zipper-flap finished edges away from the stitching. Turn right side out through the flap lower edge; press.

CONSTRUCTING THE SIDE POCKET

1. With an outer fabric pocket and a lining pocket right sides together, stitch along one short edge. Turn so wrong sides are facing; press. Insert an elastic strip between the fabrics, aligning the elastic with the seamline. Stitch the elastic ends to tack them in place. Stitch just below the elastic to create a casing, stretching the elastic as you sew. Repeat for the second pocket.

2. Fold the lower edge of the outer fabric pocket 1" toward the right side; press. To box the pocket lower edge, draw a diagonal line across the fold from each upper-edge point to ½" from the long edge on either side (fig. D). Stitch along each line. Trim the corners ⅛" from the seam; turn right side out. Repeat with the lining pocket. Tuck the fashion fabric pocket lower edge into the lining fabric lower edge. Repeat to box the second pocket lower edge. Set the pockets aside.

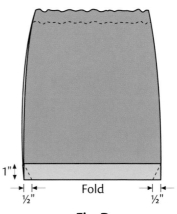

Fig. D
Box pocket lower edge.

3. Place one fabric side piece wrong side up on a flat surface. Center a corresponding stiff-interfacing rectangle over the fabric; machine baste or use temporary spray adhesive to secure the interfacing. Repeat for the remaining side. Right sides together, baste a pocket to a side, aligning the lower edges. Stop sewing ½" from the corners. Repeat to stitch the remaining pocket. (The pocket lining is now on the outside.)

CONSTRUCTING THE BODY

1. Machine baste one stiff-interfacing body piece to one fabric-body piece wrong side. Pin the hook side of the hook-

and-loop tape 1¼" from the body-piece upper edge and 2" from each short edge. Satin stitch around the hook piece through all layers. (The stiff interfacing helps stabilize the fabric.) This piece is now the bag back.

2. Place the remaining fabric body right side down on a flat surface. Center the small batting rectangle over the fabric. Machine baste or use temporary spray adhesive to secure the batting. Center the remaining stiff-interfacing body piece over the batting; machine baste. This is now the bag front.

3. Machine baste the stiff-interfacing base to the fabric base.

CONSTRUCTING THE TIES, TABS & STRAPS

1. Fold each tab in half with right sides together; press. Stitch one short end and the long edge. Turn each tube right side out and press the seam so it's centered on the back. Fold each tab in half widthwise, press, and then unfold.

2. Align the straight bar of one small D-ring with one backpack-tab pressed fold. Fold the backpack tab around the D-ring with the seams facing. Baste close to the D-ring. Repeat for the remaining backpack tab.

3. Align the straight bar of one large D-ring with one tab foldline. Fold the tab around the D-ring with the seams facing. Baste close to the D-ring. Repeat for the remaining tabs.

4. Fold each strap in half lengthwise with right sides together. Stitch the long edge. Turn the straps right side out and press so the seam is centered on the back.

5. Thread one backpack-strap end through a snap hook. Turn under the raw edge 1", and then stitch close to the fold to encase the snap hook, stitching as close to the snap hook as the presser foot allows.

6. Thread the other strap end through the single bar, through another snap hook, and then through the middle single-bar slot (fig. E). Fold under the raw end and stitch close to the fold. Repeat to create the remaining backpack strap and messenger strap.

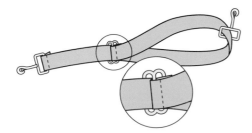

Fig. E
Thread strap end through single bar,
snap hook, and middle single-bar slot.

7. Fold each tie in half lengthwise with right sides together. Stitch the long edge and one short end. Turn the ties right side out, and then press so the seam is at one side.

8. Pin the backpack tabs (with D-rings) along the bag back upper edge, placing them ½" on both sides of the center. Align the raw edges.

9. Center one tab (with D-ring) on a side upper-edge center; align the raw edges and pin. Repeat to center and pin another tab to the remaining side. Set the remaining tabs (with D-rings) aside.

10. Pin one tie to the front upper-edge center, aligning the raw edges. Set the other tie aside.

ATTACHING THE CHANGING PAD & FLAP

1. Place the bag back and base right sides together, aligning the long edge opposite the hook piece with one base long edge. With the vinyl side of the changing pad facing the bag back right side, sandwich the changing-pad raw edge between the aligned edges; pin generously. Fold the changing pad in thirds and join the hook-and-loop tape to ensure a proper fit; adjust the changing-pad fit if needed. Unfold the changing pad.

2. Insert the remaining tabs (with D-rings) between the changing pad and base, placing them 2" from the lower-edge corners; pin (fig. F). Stitch carefully through all layers; backstitch over each strap placement.

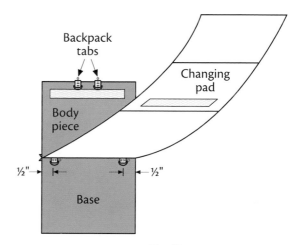

Fig. F
Attach changing pad between body and base.

3. Right sides together, pin one fabric-side piece to the back and base; stitch (fig. G). Repeat to attach the remaining fabric side.

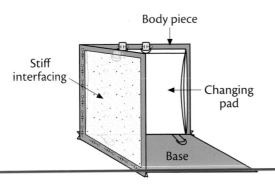

Stiff interfacing

Body piece

Changing pad

Base

Fig. G
Attach sides to back and base.

4. Pin the front to the fabric sides and base; stitch.

5. Turn the bag right side out. Fold the upper edges ½" toward the wrong side and press from the right side. Unfold the upper edge.

6. With right sides together, align the flap raw edge with the back-body upper edge. Stitch, encasing the backpack tabs in the stitching.

7. Remove the back-body basting stitches. Refold the upper edge toward the wrong side; re-press if necessary.

8. Pin the remaining tie to the back upper-edge center over the flap wrong side, aligning the raw edges. Stitch to secure following the previous stitching line.

CONSTRUCTING THE BODY LINING

1. Place one lining-body piece and the lining base right sides together, aligning one long edge. Stitch the long edge. This is now the lining back.

2. Pin one lining side to the lining back, aligning the base with one lining-side short edge; stitch. Repeat to stitch the remaining lining side to the lining back.

3. With right sides together, pin the remaining lining-body piece to the lining back, aligning the side long edges with the body-piece short edges and the base long edge with the body-piece lower edge; stitch.

4. Clip the corners, and then press open the seams. Turn the lining-body piece upper edge ½" toward the wrong side and press.

FINISHING

1. Insert the lining into the bag so wrong sides are facing. Align the corners and upper-edge folds. Pin generously around the bag upper edge. Carefully hand or machine stitch around the upper edge, close to each fold. Remove any remaining basting stitches.

2. Attach the desired straps by clipping them to the corresponding D-rings. Adjust the straps to fit.

LEAFY TOTE

Designed by Ellen March

MAKE A BEACH TOTE out of leaf-patterned cottons to make every outing feel like a vacation.

Finished size: 19½" x 16½" x 5" (excluding straps)

SUPPLIES

Yardages are based on 44"/45"-wide fabric.

- 1 yard of leaf-patterned cotton fabric for bag exterior
- 1 yard of leafy-patterned fabric for boxing strip
- 2 yards of fusible interfacing
- 3 yards of nylon webbing for straps
- 1½ yards of ¼"-wide matching ribbon for drawstring
- Matching all-purpose thread

Source

Seattle Fabrics (www.seattlefabrics.com, 866-925-0670) supplied the nylon web.

tip

If you want to use up ribbon from your stash for the straps, omit the nylon webbing. Make sure the ribbon is at least 1" wide to ensure stability.

CUTTING

From the leaf-patterned fabric, cut four 18" x 20" rectangles for the bag body.

From the solid coordinating fabric, cut two 5½" x 57" rectangles (piece the fabric if needed to achieve the required dimensions) for the boxing strip.

From the interfacing, cut two 5½" x 57" rectangles.

From the nylon webbing, cut two 54" lengths.

CONSTRUCTING THE TOTE

Sew with right sides together and a ¼" seam allowance unless otherwise noted.

1. Fuse one interfacing rectangle to each boxing-strip rectangle wrong side.

2. Position one strap along one body rectangle, aligning the strap ends with the rectangle lower raw edge (pick one long edge as the lower edge) and placing the strap outer edges 5" from the body sides; pin. Repeat to pin the second strap to one of the remaining body rectangles. Stitch each strap in place along both webbing edges, beginning and ending 2" from each rectangle upper edge (fig. A).

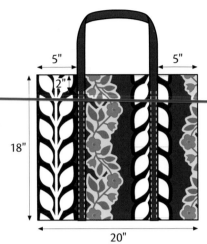

Fig. A
Stitch strap to body rectangle.

3. Pin one boxing-strip long edge to one body rectangle (with strap) along the side and lower edges. Begin and end pinning at the side upper edges. Clip the boxing strip at each corner to ease it around the body square. Stitch the boxing strip to the rectangle. Pin the opposite boxing-strip long edge to a second body square (with strap) in the same manner; stitch. Turn the body right side out.

4. Repeat to pin and stitch the remaining boxing strip to the remaining two body rectangles (without straps); leave a 5" opening along one lower edge. This forms the lining.

5. Insert the main body inside the lining body. Align the seams and upper edges; pin, making sure the straps are tucked inside and away from the stitching line. Stitch along the upper edge.

6. Turn the tote right side out through the lining opening. Slipstitch the opening closed. Push the lining inside the main body and press the upper edge. Edgestitch along the upper edge.

7. Fold the upper edge 1" toward the wrong side; press. Be careful to avoid pressing over the nylon webbing straps. Unfold the upper edge. Pin-mark the center point along one side of the upper edge ½" below the foldline (fig. B).

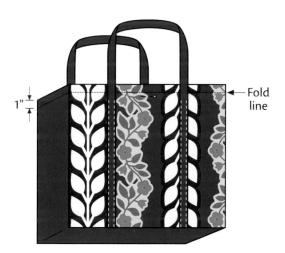

Fig. B
Pin-mark buttonhole placement.

tip

• Find sailboat- or seashell-print fabric and use rope as the drawstring for a nautical-inspired bag.
• Try using Hawaiian cottons to make every outing feel like a tropical vacation.

8. Stitch a ½"-wide horizontal buttonhole at the pin mark. Apply seam sealant to the buttonhole if desired; cut open the buttonhole.

9. Refold the tote upper edge along the foldline. Stitch, following the previous stitching line to create a casing. Stitch across the straps along the tote upper edge (fig. C).

Fig. C
Stitch over straps at tote upper edge.

10. Pin a safety pin to one ribbon end. Insert the safety pin in the buttonhole and feed the ribbon through the casing. Use the safety pin to ease the ribbon through the casing and back out through the buttonhole. Tie a knot in each ribbon end, and then tie the ribbon into a bow.

SAILBOAT TOTE

Designed by Beth Bradley

NAUTICAL-THEMED APPAREL AND ACCESSORIES are spring fashion classics, so you'll see this preppy look on the runway and in ready-to-wear. Using water-repellent, fade-resistant outdoor fabric, make a trendy nautical tote that's stylish, sensible and sturdy. You'll be all set for sailing the high seas.

Finished tote size: 16" x 10" (excluding straps)

SUPPLIES

Yardages are based on 60"-wide fabric.

- ½ yard of water-repellent, fade-resistant canvas, such as Sunbrella (fabric A)
- ¼ yard of contrasting color canvas (fabric B)
- Size 16/100 or 18/110 sewing machine needle
- Four 1½"-diameter drapery grommets
- Matching heavyweight thread
- Air-soluble fabric-marking pen

Source

Beacon Fabric and Notions (www.beaconfabric.com, 800-713-8157) provided the Mediterranean blue and parchment Sunbrella canvas and the 1½" polished silver drapery grommets.

CUTTING

From fabric A, cut two 14" x 17" rectangles and two 3" x 30" strips.

From fabric B, cut two 2" x 17" strips and two 1" x 17" strips.

CONSTRUCTING THE TOTE

Sew with right sides together and a ½" seam allowance unless otherwise noted.

1. Position one fabric A rectangle right side up (choose one 17" edge as the lower edge). Position one 2" x 17" fabric B strip right side up over the rectangle, 6½" down from the rectangle upper edge. Align the strip with the rectangle side edges; pin. Position one 1" x 17" fabric B strip right side up 1" below the first strip; pin (fig. A). Repeat with the other fabric A rectangle.

Fig. A
Position fabric strips.

2. Using a decorative or wide zigzag stitch, stitch along each fabric B strip long edge to secure it to the fabric A rectangle.

3. Serge the rectangle lower and side edges (or use an overedge or zigzag stitch).

4. Fold one rectangle upper edge ½" toward the wrong side; press. Sew a ¼" hem. Fold again 2½" toward the wrong side; press. Stitch 2¼" from the upper fold edge; press. Edgestitch along the rectangle upper edge (fig. B). Repeat with the other rectangle.

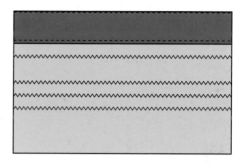

Fig. B
Edgestitch along upper folded edge.

5. Pin the two rectangles together. Stitch them together along the side and lower edges.

6. Box the tote lower corners, stitching 1½" from the triangle point. Cut off the triangle ½" from the stitching; serge- or zigzag-finish the raw edges. Turn the bag right side out. Use a knitting needle to push out the corners. (See "Asian Purse-uasion" on page 65 for a helpful illustration.)

7. Mark 5½" from each rectangle side edge and 1¼" down from the upper edge (fig. C). This mark will be the center of the circle that you'll cut out for each grommet. Follow the grommet manufacturer's instructions to install the four grommets (two on each tote side).

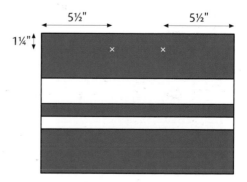

Fig. C
Mark center of grommet circles.

8. For each 3" x 30" fabric A strip, fold ¼" toward the fabric wrong side along the long edges; press. Wrong sides facing, fold each strip in half; press (fig. D).

Fig. D
Fold strip in half.

9. To create the tote shoulder straps, edgestitch along each folded strip long edge. Serge each strap short end.

10. Insert the strap ends through the grommet holes from the outside of the tote. Pull the straps through approximately 3" to the tote inside. Fold up the 3" end to meet the outside strap portion to form a loop. Stitch slowly (the fabric layers are very thick at this point) across the strap ½" from the strap end (fig. E). Repeat to secure the straps through the remaining three grommets.

Fig. E
Stitch across strap ends.

HEAVY DUTY

Sunbrella and other types of heavyweight outdoor fabrics require special tricks for smooth sewing:

- Use a longer stitch length (3.0 mm to 4.0 mm).

- Use a size 16/100 or 18/110 needle.

- Choose a project with uncomplicated style lines.

- Use sharp scissors for cutting curves and a rotary cutter and mat for cutting straight lines.

- Use a heavier thread, such as thread for sewing on denim, or V69 thread, available at beaconfabric.com.

- Make sure the hardware that you've selected is sturdy enough to support the fabric.

- Test-sew on a scrap of the outdoor fabric to see if you need to adjust your machine's tension before you start the project.

ROPED IN

Make straps for this tote out of nylon webbing or cotton rope instead of fabric.

LET'S DO LUNCH

Designed by Shannon Dennis

STITCH A COLORFUL LUNCH BAG that you can take to school
or the office and use again and again.

Finished bag size: approximately 10" x 13"

SUPPLIES

Yardages are based on 44"/45"-wide fabric.

- ½ yard of solid fabric for bag exterior
- ½ yard of print fabric with motifs you can cut out for lining, tabs and embellishments
- ⅓ yard of insulated batting (such as Insul-Bright)
- ¼ yard of stiff fusible interfacing (such as fast2fuse)
- ¾" button
- Matching cotton sewing thread
- Matching or contrasting decorative thread
- Spray adhesive

CUTTING

From the solid fabric, cut one 11" x 28" rectangle for the bag.

From the print fabric, cut one 11" x 28" rectangle for the lining and two 2½" x 7" rectangles for the tab.

From the insulated batting, cut one 11" x 28" rectangle.

From the stiff fusible interfacing, cut one 4" x 6" rectangle for the bag bottom.

CONSTRUCTING THE BAG

Sew with right sides together and a ¼" seam allowance unless otherwise noted.

1. Center the insulated batting on the bag fabric rectangle wrong side; pin. Using the decorative thread and decorative stitches or free-motion stitching, stitch all over the rectangle to secure the layers together.

2. Square up the stitched rectangle. Fold the rectangle in half widthwise so it measures approximately 11" x 14"; pin. Stitch the long edges.

3. Box the bag corners, stitching 2" from the triangle points. Cut off the triangles ¼" from the stitching; serge- or zigzag-finish the seams. Press open. Repeat to box the opposite corner. (See "Asian Purse-uasion" on page 65 for a helpful illustration.)

4. Fold the lining rectangle in half widthwise so it measures approximately 11" x 14"; pin. Stitch the long edges. Box the corners as directed for the bag fabric rectangle.

5. Right sides together, pin the lining and bag together around the upper raw edge. Stitch, leaving a 4" opening for turning.

6. Turn the bag right side out through the opening and stuff the lining into the bag. Extend the lining over the bag upper edge approximately ½" to produce a binding effect. Use a zigzag or other decorative stitch to sew around the upper edge, closing the opening with the stitching (fig. A).

Fig. A

7. To make the tab, stitch the two 2½" x 7" print fabric rectangles together along the perimeter. Leave an opening along one lengthwise edge for turning. Turn the tab right side out; press. Whipstitch the opening closed.

8. Stitch a buttonhole at one end of the tab, centering it ¾" from the end. Fold under the opposite tab end ½"; pin (fig. B).

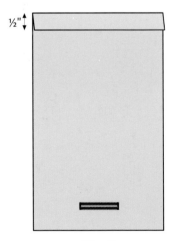

½"

Fig. B

9. Align the bag side seams to find the bag center back; pin-mark. Center the tab folded end on the lunch bag center back; stitch.

10. Fold over the bag and mark where the buttonhole hits the bag. Hand or machine sew a button at the mark.

11. Cut out a motif from the print fabric. Spray the motif wrong side with spray adhesive. Wrong sides facing, align the motif with a scrap of the solid fabric. Cut out the motif. Print side up, position the motif on the bag center back, covering the tab end; stitch.

Add free-motion stitching to the entire bag or just to portions, as on the featured bag. Experiment with different stitches, designs and threads before stitching the actual project.

GYM SACK

Designed by Joan Vardanega

THIS SIMPLE, STURDY NYLON BAG doubles as a backpack. Stash your
gear inside for trips to the gym or your next sports practice.

Finished size: approximately 15" x 18"

SUPPLIES

- ½ yard of 54"- to 60"-wide nylon fabric for bag (200-400 denier nylon suggested)
- 4 yards of ³/₁₆"-diameter nylon cording
- Matching or contrasting polyester thread
- 1 yard of double-fold bias or twill tape
- 2¼" square of stiff fabric (such as Ultrasuede)
- Two ⅜" metal grommets and grommet-setting tool
- Size 14 or 16 Sharp, Jeans or Microtex sewing-machine needle
- Fabric-marking pen
- Large paper clips or binder clips
- Large safety pin or bodkin

Source

Rose City Textiles (www.rosecitytextiles.com) provided the nylon fabric and cording.

CUTTING

From the nylon, cut one 16" x 40" rectangle.

CONSTRUCTING THE BAG

1. Fold the nylon rectangle in half widthwise, right sides together. Position the folded rectangle on a flat work surface with the folded edge as the lower edge.

2. Draw a line 3" from the upper edge. On each side edge, make a small mark ⅜" above the 3" line (fig. A). Turn over the folded rectangle and mark the other fabric wrong side in the same manner.

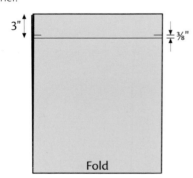

Fig. A
Mark folded fabric.

3. Paperclip the rectangle side edges together. Using a ⅝" seam allowance, stitch the rectangle side edges from

each ⅜" mark to the folded edge. Clip the seam allowance at the ⅜" mark.

4. Press open the seam allowances above the clips. Topstitch the seam allowances close to the folded edges (fig. B).

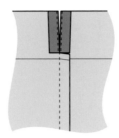

Fig. B
Topstitch seam allowances.

5. Cut a piece of bias tape that's approximately 18" long. Beginning below the clip, enclose the seam allowance in the bias tape fold. Fold the bias tape short edge ½" toward the tape wrong side to enclose the seam allowance raw upper edge; paperclip in place (fig. C). The bias tape length will end a few inches above the bag folded edge; this reduces bulk at the bag corners. Zigzag the bias tape in place. Repeat to enclose the other seam allowance.

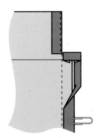

Fig. C
Place bias tape over
seam allowances.

6. On each bag side, stitch a line ½" from the upper edge. Use this stitching line as a guide to fold the bag upper edges ½" toward the fabric wrong side. Paperclip in place. Stitch ⅜" from each folded edge (fig. D).

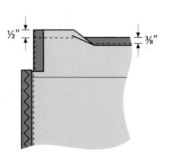

Fig. D
Stitch ⅜" from folded edge.

7. To create the cording casing, fold one bag upper edge down to meet the marked line (from step 2). Paperclip in place. Stitch ⅛" from the fold (fig. E). Don't stitch past the side seams. Repeat to create the casing on the other bag side.

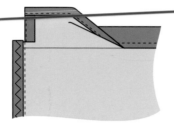

Fig. E
Fold down to marked line; stitch.

8. At the bag lower corners, trim the seam allowances on the diagonal. Turn the bag right side out.

9. Cut the stiff fabric square in half diagonally so that you have two triangles. On one bag right side, position a triangle on each bag lower corner, aligning the triangle edges ⅛" from the bag edges. Paperclip the triangles in place. Stitch around the triangle perimeters. With the stiff fabric side facing down, install one grommet in each triangle according to the grommet tool manufacturer's instructions (fig. F).

Fig. F
Install grommets.

10. Cut the nylon cording in half. To finish the cording ends, sear the edges with a flame. Hold the cording end near a candle flame just until the nylon begins to melt.

11. Attach the bodkin or safety pin about ½" from the cording end. Thread the safety pin right to left through the front and back casings (fig. G). Remove the safety pin from the cording.

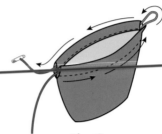

Fig. G
Thread cording right to left through casing.

12. Attach the safety pin to the other cording piece end. Thread the cording through the front casing and back casing in the opposite direction (fig. H).

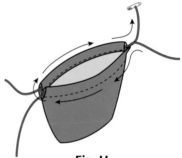

Fig. H
Thread right cording left to right through casing.

13. Match the cut ends of one cording piece. Thread both cording ends through one grommet from back to front (stiff fabric side). Tie the cording ends together in an overhand knot; tie a double knot if necessary. Repeat to secure the other cording piece through the other grommet (fig. I).

Fig. I
Thread cording through grommets; knot.

MESH
BEACH
TOTE

Designed by Ellen March

MAKE A BEACH TOTE OUT OF MESH FABRIC so you can easily shake away the sand from your towel, flip-flops, book and water bottle—without even opening the bag!

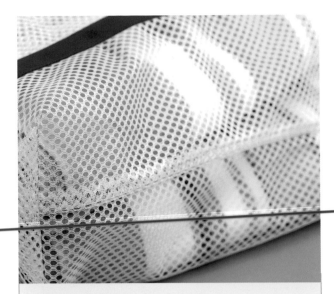

CUTTING

From the mesh, cut one 20" x 40" rectangle for the body and one 9" x 18" rectangle for the pocket.

From the webbing, cut one 9" length for the pocket upper edge. Set aside the remainder for the strap. Carefully use a match to sear the webbing ends to prevent fraying.

CONSTRUCTING THE TOTE

Sew with a ½" seam allowance unless otherwise noted.

1. Fold the body rectangle in half widthwise; pin-mark along the fold. Place the body rectangle flat on your work surface with the pins facing up.

2. Position the webbing strap over the rectangle. Pin one strap seared end along the pin-marked center, with the strap long edge 5" from one mesh long edge. At the mesh short edge, loop 30" of strap and continue to pin the strap to the body along the opposite side. Create another strap loop at the opposite mesh short end, and then continue to pin the strap until the seared edges are aligned (fig. A).

MESH MASH

Mesh fabric that has coarse openings feeds better through a conventional sewing machine if you:

• Use a short stitch length.

• Use a narrow zigzag stitch rather than a straight stitch.

• Use a tear-away, wash-away or tissue-paper stabilizer underneath so the feed dogs aren't grabbing air; remove the stabilizer after sewing.

• Place the mesh layer on top and next to the needle when stitching it to another fabric.

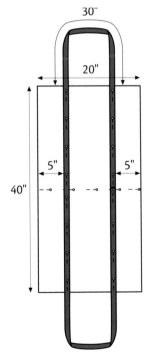

Fig. A
Pin strap in place.

3. Fold the pocket rectangle in half widthwise. Position the 9" webbing strip on the edge opposite the fold, concealing the raw edges; pin. Stitch the webbing to the pocket along both webbing long edges (fig. B).

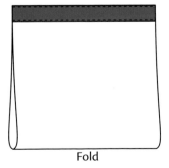

Fold

Fig. B
Stitch webbing to pocket upper edge.

4. Position the pocket on the body, aligning the pocket fold with the mesh center pin-marks. Tuck the pocket side edges under the strap edges; repin the straps over the pocket if needed. Remove the pins along the body center.

5. Stitch the strap to the body along both webbing edges, beginning and ending 2" from each mesh short edge (fig. C). Remove the pins as you sew.

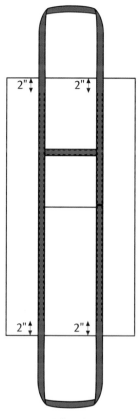

Fig. C
Stitch strap in place.

6. Fold the tote in half widthwise with right sides together. Stitch the side seams, and then zigzag the seams together for a stronger finish.

7. Box the tote corners, stitching 2" from the triangle points. Cut off the triangle ½" from the stitching; serge- or zigzag-finish the seams. (See "Asian Purse-uasion" on page 65 for a helpful illustration.)

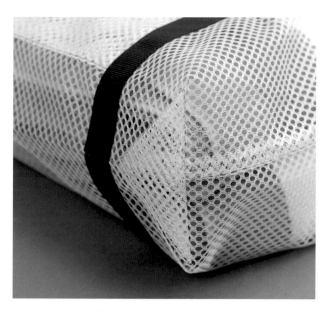

Boxed corners give the tote dimension.

8. Turn the tote right side out. Double-fold the tote upper edge 1" toward the wrong side; pin. Stitch along the second fold.

tip

To clean, empty the tote and hose it off—it's just that easy!

HIT THE BOOKS

Designed by Ellen March

TRANSFORM FUN COORDINATING
PRINT FABRICS into a messenger bag that's
full of pockets to hold everything you need.
The canvas interlining makes it durable
enough to withstand years of wear
and tear.

Finished size: 13¾" x 14"

SUPPLIES

Yardages are based on 44"/45"-wide fabric.

- 1 yard of print fabric (fabric A) for bag
- ½ yard each of 2 coordinating print fabrics (fabrics B & C) for lining and strap
- ¾ yard of mediumweight white or tan canvas for pocket
- 15"-long piece of ½"-wide elastic
- Coordinating 12" zipper
- Matching all-purpose thread

Source

The Fat Quarter Shop (www.fatquartershop.com, 866-826-2069) provided the Michael Miller Funky Christmas coordinating print fabrics.

CUTTING

From fabric A, cut one 15" square and one 18" x 20" rectangle for the front panel, two 15" x 18" rectangles and two 7" x 15" rectangles for the back panel, and four 3" squares for the zipper tabs.

From fabric B, cut one 15" square for the front panel lining and one 15" x 25" rectangle for the back panel lining.

From fabric C, cut two 6" x 44" strips for the strap and two 7½" x 10" rectangles for the pocket.

From the canvas, cut two 2½" x 42" strips for the strap and one 15" square for the front panel.

CONSTRUCTING THE PANELS

Sew with right sides together and a ¼" seam allowance unless otherwise noted.

1. Fold the front panel rectangle widthwise with wrong sides together; press. Topstitch ⅛" from the fold. Stitch ⅝" from the topstitching to create a casing for the elastic.

2. Insert the elastic through the casing; pin one elastic end to one casing end. Ease the fabric around the elastic to evenly distribute the gathers. Pin the opposite elastic end to the opposite casing end.

3. Mark three equidistant dots along the elastic panel lower edge. Draw a 2"-long line 1" from each dot on either side (fig. A).

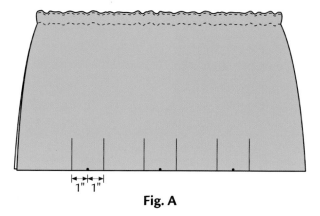

Fig. A

4. Match the lines surrounding each dot, and then press to create box pleats (fig. B). Set aside the elastic panel.

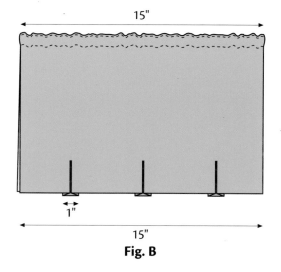

Fig. B

5. Position the canvas square on a flat work surface. Position the fabric A square over the canvas with the right side facing up. Position the elastic panel right side over the fabric A square, aligning the edges.

6. With right sides together, position the fabric B square over the stacked elastic panel, front panel and canvas square. Stitch around the perimeter, using a ½" seam allowance. Leave a 4" opening along the lower edge for turning. Stitch the front panel perimeter again, following the previous stitching line, to reinforce the heavy layers.

7. Turn the front panel right side out through the opening. Press the opening edges closed. Set aside the front panel.

8. With right sides together, stitch the fabric C pocket rectangles along the short edges and one long edge. Turn the pocket right side out. Fold the raw edges ¼" toward the wrong side; press. The open edge is the lower edge.

9. Using a removable fabric marker, draw four vertical lines across the pocket width, with the first line 1¼" from the pocket right-side edge. Leave 1¼" between each pocket divider line (fig. C).

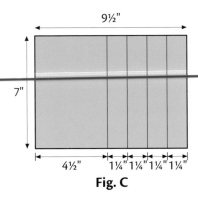

Fig. C

10. Position two zipper tabs with right sides together. Sandwich the zipper end between the tabs, aligning the ends. Stitch ½" from the end, stitching slowly over the zipper coils (fig. D). Fold the tabs so the right sides are facing out; finger-press.

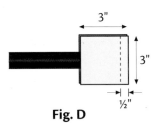

Fig. D

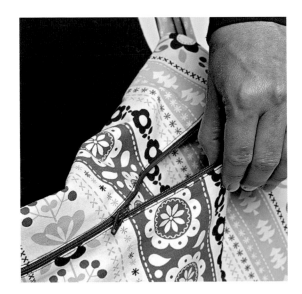

11. Unzip the zipper partway to keep the zipper pull away from the presser foot. Abut the zipper teeth along the zipper top; pin. Stitch the remaining zipper tabs to the zipper top, following the instructions for the zipper end.

12. Trim the zipper tabs even with the zipper upper and lower edges.

13. Fold one long edge of each fabric A short rectangle ¼" toward the wrong side; press. Fold one short edge of each fabric A long rectangle ¼" toward the wrong side; press.

14. Position the short rectangles wrong sides together, aligning the folds. Insert the zipper lower edge between the short rectangles; stitch close to the zipper teeth using a zipper foot (fig. E).

Fig. E

15. Position the large rectangles wrong sides together, aligning the folds. Insert the zipper upper edge between the large rectangles; stitch close to the teeth using a zipper foot.

16. Trim the zipper tab ends even with the panel edges.

17. Position the pocket over the fabric B back panel with the pocket lower edge centered 2" from one back panel short edge. Topstitch the pocket sides and lower edge, closing the open pocket edge with the stitching. Leave the pocket upper edge free. Stitch along each pocket divider line, backstitching at the beginning and ending of each stitching line.

18. Position the fabric B back panel over the fabric A back panel with right sides together, all edges aligned and the zipper edge opposite the pocket edge. Stitch the back panel perimeter, and then turn it right side out through the zipper. Zip the zipper closed.

19. With right sides together, stitch the fabric strips along one end using a ¼" seam allowance; press open the seam. Repeat to stitch the canvas strips.

20. Fold one fabric strip end ¼" toward the wrong side; press. Fold the fabric strip in half lengthwise with right sides together; press. Stitch the long edge. Turn the strap right side out using a tube turner, chopstick or knitting needle.

21. Center the seam along one side; press. The seam side is the wrong side.

22. Pin a safety pin to one canvas strip end. Insert the pinned end through the strap, distributing the fabric around the canvas strip until each canvas end is ⅝" from the strap ends. Make sure the strip isn't twisted. Re-press if needed.

23. Push the raw strap end ⅝" into the folded strap end, making sure the strap isn't twisted. Stitch close to the fold through all layers (fig. F).

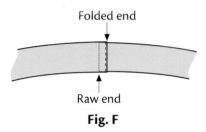

Fig. F

ASSEMBLING THE BAG

1. Position the back panel on a flat work surface with fabric B facing up. Position the front panel fabric B side over the back panel, aligning the lower edges. Draw a horizontal line on the back panel lining to mark the front-panel upper edge placement (fig. G). Stitch the back panel along the line.

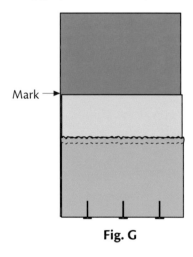

Fig. G

2. With right sides together, align the strap seam with the front panel lower-edge center. Pin the front panel to the strap, easing the strap around the corners. Stitch the strap to the front panel sides and lower edge using a scant ¼" seam allowance (fig. H). Backstitch at the panel upper edges.

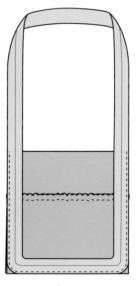

Fig. H

3. With right sides together, align the strap seam with the back panel lower-edge center. Pin the back panel to the strap, easing the strap around the corners. Stitch the strap to the back panel lower edge and sides, ending the stitching and backstitching when the back panel horizontal stitching lines are reached.

4. Turn the messenger bag right side out. Fold the zippered flap over the front panel.

READY-TO-WEAR TOTES

Designed by Pauline Richards

WHETHER YOU ACCIDENTALLY LAUNDER a favorite wool sweater or purchase a sweater to felt, you'll enjoy making and using these one-of-a-kind handbags.

Finished tote size: approximately 16" x 13"

SUPPLIES

- Size large (or larger) 100% wool sweater with 3"-wide contrasting ribbing, felted and pressed (see "Felting for Success" below), for tote exterior*
- ½ yard of 45"-wide fabric for lining
- 2½" x 45" rectangle of coordinating faux suede
- 8" x 12" rectangle of double-sided fusible web (such as Steam-A-Seam 2)
- 16" metal zipper
- 5" length of ¼"-wide ribbon
- Matching all-purpose thread

The featured black-and-white bag began as a men's size extra-large sweater.

FELTING FOR SUCCESS

Felting occurs when 100% wool or a combination of wool and other fibers are agitated in hot soapy water. The soap removes the lanolin, a natural lubricant and by-product of wool. Once the lanolin is removed, the barbs on the individual fibers lock together and tighten, and the heat aids in shrinking the fibers to create felt.

Felting is permanent, so be cautious. To ensure the desired results, agitate for about 10 minutes and then check the amount of shrinkage. Continue agitating, checking the fabric every five to 10 minutes. When you're happy with the shrinkage, rinse well, squeeze out the excess water, and lay flat to dry. If more shrinkage is desired, dry on low heat or wash again in hot water. Before cutting, cover the sweater with a press cloth and steam press.

Sweaters felt differently according to fiber content, agitation time and original size, so check the fiber content before beginning a felted project. When searching for wool to felt, look for a sweater that contains at least 90% wool. The higher the percentage of animal fiber, the more felting will occur. Avoid garments labeled "washable wool." Washable wools are treated with a resin finish and won't felt. Don't use them for this project.

CUTTING

From the sweater, cut out the bag according to the measurements provided (fig. A). The sweater side seams become the bag side seams. These measurements are only a guideline. Size the bag larger or smaller as desired to best utilize the sweater you're working with.

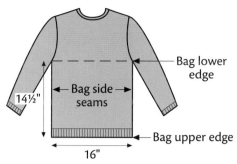

Bag lower edge

14½"

Bag side seams

Bag upper edge

16"

Fig. A
Cut bag from felted sweater.

From the lining fabric, cut one 16" x 23" rectangle, or customize the lining dimensions to fit the bag you've cut.

CONSTRUCTING THE TOTE

Sew with right sides together and a ½" seam allowance unless otherwise noted.

1. Fold the lining in half to create an 11½" x 16" rectangle. Stitch the short edges together (fig. B). Fold the lining upper edge ½" to the wrong side; press.

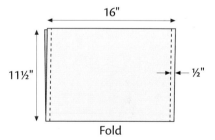

16"

11½"

½"

Fold

Fig. B
Fold and stitch lining.

2. Stitch the bag lower edge, leaving a 5" opening for turning. If you cut the bag smaller than the felted sweater width, stitch the side seams.

3. Box the bag and lining lower corners, stitching 1½" from the triangle points. Cut off the triangle ½" from the stitching; serge- or zigzag-finish the seams. Turn the bag right side out. (See "Asian Purse-uasian" on page 65 for a helpful illustration.)

4. Fold the ribbing in half to the wrong side; press. Edgestitch to secure.

7. Pin the handles to the bag wrong side. Stitch, following the previous ribbing stitch line and securing the handles in the process. Edgestitch along the ribbing upper edge, securing the handles again with the stitching (fig. D).

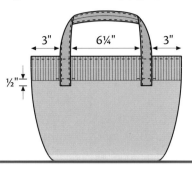

Fig. D
Edgestitch ribbing upper edge;
secure handles.

8. Unzip the zipper and place one side of the open zipper right side down along the ribbing stitch line; stitch (fig. E). Secure the remaining zipper half to the opposite side of the bag. Approximately 2" of excess zipper will remain loose and unstitched; the excess will tuck between the bag and lining when the bag is turned right side out.

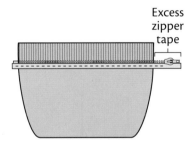

Fig. E
Attach zipper.

9. With right sides together, slip the bag inside the lining. Match the lining's folded upper edge to the zipper stitching; pin in place. Machine stitch to secure.

Add a bright lining so that you can easily see the bag contents.

Use a felted sleeve for a pocket. Apply the pocket where desired prior to construction. Use binding or ribbon to cover the raw edges and add a decorative effect.

5. To create handles, cut and fuse 2¼"-wide strips of fusible web to the 2½" x 45" faux-suede rectangle. Remove the paper backing. Fold the long raw edges to meet at the center back, encasing the fusible web strips; fuse (fig. C).

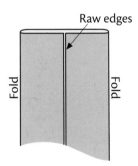

Fig. C
Create handles.

6. Topstitch ¼" and ⅜" from the folded edges, and then cut the strip in half to create two 22½"-long handles.

10. Turn the bag right side out through the bag opening. Fold in the opening edges and hand stitch to close. Tie the ribbon through the zipper pull.

SWEATER SMARTS

Thrift stores are a great sweater source. Look in all departments and don't overlook sweaters that appear accidentally felted. These rare finds enable you to skip the felting process and go right to cutting and sewing. When constructing the bag, consider the following:

- Add body to the bag by sewing heavyweight interfacing to the felted fabric wrong side.

- Utilize existing buttonholes to incorporate unique design elements. Choose fun new buttons and hand sew them in place after felting the sweater. Close the front sweater opening with hand-sewn blanket stitches.

- Instead of faux suede, use nylon webbing or a sturdy trim for handles.

REUSABLE GROCERY BAG

Designed by Beth Bradley

DO YOUR PART TO HELP THE PLANET and just say "no" to plastic shopping bags. Use recycled nylon fabric to sew an eco-friendly alternative. This sturdy, water-resistant and lightweight tote folds up to fit in your purse or pocket for trips to the farmer's market or grocery store.

SUPPLIES

- Salvaged nylon fabric (look for nylon windbreakers, tents or gym bags)
- Matching all-purpose or polyester thread

CUTTING

From the nylon fabric, cut out the bag and facing pieces using the patterns on page 43 (enlarge patterns 200%). Cut one 4" x 41¾" strip for the gusset (depending on the size of garment or item you've salvaged, you may need to piece the gusset strip to achieve the required length).

CONSTRUCTING THE BAG

Sew with right sides together and a ½" seam allowance unless otherwise noted.

1. Serge- or zigzag-finish one facing lower edge (fig. A).

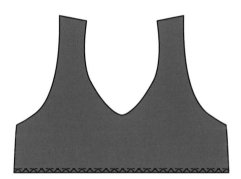

Fig. A
Serge facing lower edge.

2. With wrong sides facing, pin one pair of bag pieces together along the center front edge. Stitch a flat-fell seam (see "Flat-Fell Seams" on page 42) at the bag center front.

3. Position one tote facing over the constructed tote side, aligning the upper edges; pin. Stitch the upper curved edges and straight side edges (fig. B); do not stitch across the handle edges. Press the seam allowances toward the facing. Clip the seam allowances around the curves.

Fig. B
Stitch upper and side edges.

THRIFTY TIPS

When searching the thrift store for fabric to repurpose, keep these tips in mind.

- Make note of the instructions on the original garment care label.
- Garments or items that have large uninterrupted areas of fabric work best for recycling into new projects.
- Use a seam ripper to deconstruct the garment and see how much fabric you have. You may need to get creative with piecing the fabric in order to cut out larger pattern pieces.

4. Turn the bag right side out. Use a knitting needle to push out the edges; press. Along the unfaced side edges, trim the bag seam allowance even with the faced edge.

5. Fold each upper handle edge ½" toward the facing side. Overlap the two folded edges; pin. Stitch across the handle close to each folded edge (fig. C).

Fig. C
Stitch handle close to each fold.

6. Repeat steps 1–5 to construct the other bag side and facing.

7. Fold each gusset short edge ⅜" toward the fabric wrong side. Fold again ½" toward the wrong side. Stitch close to the first fold.

8. Pin the gusset along one bag side and lower edges. Stitch the side and lower edges (fig. D). For more control, use the hand wheel rather than the presser foot to stitch the lower corners. Press open the side and lower seams. Repeat to attach the other bag side to the gusset.

Fig. D
Stitch gusset to bag piece.

9. Serge- or zigzag-finish the side and lower bag seams. Turn the bag right side out.

FLAT-FELL SEAMS

Flat-fell seams are used frequently in denim or athletic garment construction because they're extra tough and durable. A flat-fell seam on a grocery tote provides strength to hold all the goodies you gather.

1. Sew a ½" seam with the fabric wrong sides facing. Press open the seam.

2. Trim one seam allowance to ¼" (1). Press the trimmed seam allowance toward the wider seam allowance.

3. Fold the wider seam allowance in half, encasing the narrower seam allowance (2). Flip the seam allowance over to hide the raw edge; pin.

4. Stitch close to the folded edge (3); press.

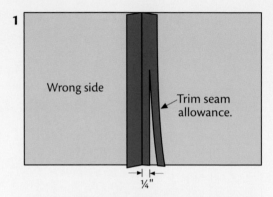

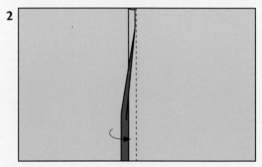

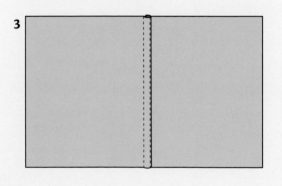

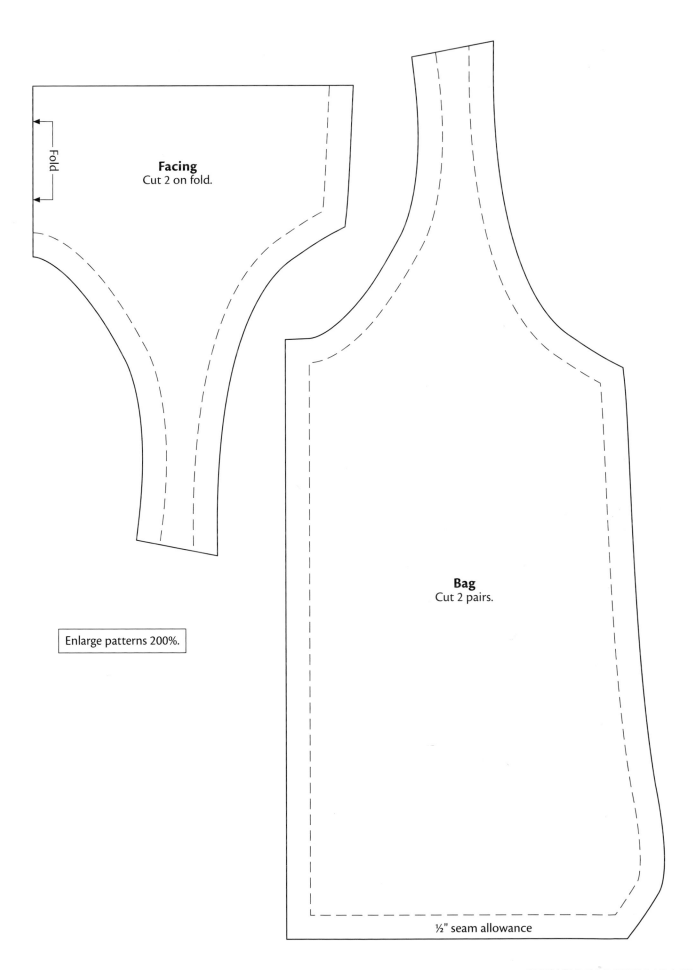

Facing
Cut 2 on fold.

Fold

Enlarge patterns 200%.

Bag
Cut 2 pairs.

½" seam allowance

ZIPPER TOTE

Designed by Linda Lee

THIS STYLISH ZIPPER TOTE holds all of your essentials securely. Choose a sturdy fabric in a striking graphic print to make a bold statement.

Finished tote size: 9½" x 12½" x 4½" (excluding straps)

SUPPLIES

Yardages are based on 44"/45"-wide fabric.

- ½ yard of heavyweight fabric, such as cotton canvas (fabric A), for tote exterior
- ⅛ yard of mediumweight contrast fabric (fabric B) for zipper flange
- Two 18½"-long pieces of 1½"-wide webbing
- One 12" decorative metal zipper
- Matching all-purpose thread

CUTTING

From fabric A, cut two 15" x 16¾" rectangles for the tote exterior.

From fabric B, cut two 3" x 8½" rectangles for the zipper flange.

CONSTRUCTING THE TOTE

Sew with right sides together and a ½" seam allowance unless otherwise noted.

1. Cut a 2¼" square from the two lower corners of each fabric A rectangle (fig. A).

Fig. A
Cut squares from lower corners.

2. Serge- or zigzag-finish one fabric A rectangle side and lower edges. Mark the center point along the rectangle upper edge. Mark 1½" to the left and right of the center mark. Pin the ends of one webbing strap to the fabric rectangle right side upper edge, aligning the strap inner edges with the outer marks. Baste across the strap ends (fig. B).

Fig. B
Baste across strap ends.

tip

Add a lining to the bag by fusing light- to mediumweight fabric to the fabric A rectangles before beginning construction.

3. To create the zipper flange, fold one 3" x 8½" strip in half lengthwise with right sides together; press. Stitch across each strip end (fig. C). Turn the strip right side out; press.

Fig. C
Stitch across strip ends.

4. Center the flange over the fabric A rectangle, aligning the flange lengthwise raw edge with the rectangle upper edge and sandwiching the strap; pin. Baste along the flange raw edge through all the layers (fig. D). Repeat steps 2 through 4 to create the other bag piece.

Fig. D
Baste along flange raw edge.

Tie the look together with a multicolor zipper.

5. Stitch the bag pieces together along the side and lower edges, leaving the lower corner cutouts open (fig. E). Press open the seams.

Fig. E
Stitch side and lower edges.

6. Pinch together one lower corner opening, matching the side and lower seams. Stitch across each corner (fig. F). Serge- or zigzag-finish the seam. Repeat to stitch the other corner.

Fig. F
Stitch across corner.

7. Serge- or zigzag-finish the bag upper edge. Fold the upper edge 1½" toward the wrong side; press.

8. Edgestitch the upper folded edge of the bag, keeping the flanges and straps out of the way. Then topstitch the bag 1" from the upper edge, this time catching the flanges and straps (fig. G).

Fig. G
Topstitch 1" from upper edge.

9. With the zipper closed and right side up, position each zipper-tape long edge underlapping each flange by about ¼". The zipper pull should be aligned about ⅛" below the flange short ends. Fold under the remaining upper zipper-tape ends to the wrong side. Pin the zipper-tape edges in place (fig. H). Unzip the zipper. Using a zipper foot, stitch the zipper tape to the flanges.

Fig. H
Pin zipper-tape edges.

10. If you're using a zipper that's longer than 12", close the zipper. Measure the zipper lower end 4½" from the flanges; mark. Cut the zipper at the mark. To finish the zipper, fold the zipper tape toward the wrong side at the cut end. Cut a fabric scrap into two 1" squares. Sandwich the zipper raw end between the two fabric squares; stitch around the square perimeter (fig. I).

Fig. I
Stitch around square.

LAUNDRY BAG

Designed by Shannon Dennis

HAULING DIRTY CLOTHES TO THE LAUNDROMAT (or your parents' house) is a breeze when you have a big laundry bag. Tuck detergent, dryer sheets and quarters into the pocket and you're ready to wash.

SUPPLIES

- 1 large bath towel (see "Open & Shut Case" below)
- ½ yard of 45"-wide cotton fabric for pocket
- Removable fabric marker
- Tube turner (optional)
- Cotton thread

CUTTING

From the cotton fabric, cut one 13½" x 27" rectangle for the pocket. From the remaining fabric, cut enough 2½"-wide strips to equal 64" in length when pieced together.

CONSTRUCTING THE BAG

1. Right sides together, fold the 13½" x 27" rectangle in half widthwise. Stitch around the edges, leaving a 4" opening along one edge for turning. Trim the corners and turn the pocket right side out. Press, turning in the opening edges; pin.

2. Wrong sides together, fold the towel in half widthwise. Center the rectangle on the bag front right side approximately 5" from the fold. Stitch around the lower and side edges to form a pocket (fig. A).

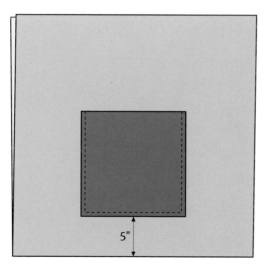

5"

Fig. A

tip

To make the bag a little more personal, use a printed T-shirt to make the pocket. Cut two 13½" squares from the T-shirt, centering the design in one square. Create the pocket as directed in step 1. For more storage, create another pocket and stitch it to the bag back.

3. Right sides together, fold the towel in half widthwise; pin. Stitch the side seams. If the towel ends already have a casing, end stitching before the openings (fig. B).

Fig. B
Stitch side seams.

4. Box the bag corners, stitching 4" from the triangle points. Cut off the triangles ¼" from the stitching; serge- or zigzag-finish the seams; press open. Repeat to box the opposite corner. (See "Asian Purse-uasion" on page 65 for a helpful illustration.)

OPEN & SHUT CASE

When you're shopping for the bath towel for this project, look for one that has a casing on each end. Then the casing is already done! If you can't find that type of towel, follow step 5 to create a casing.

5. If the towel doesn't have a casing, create one. Turn under the upper edge ½" to the wrong side; press. Turn under the upper edge 2" to the wrong side; press. Stitch close to the lower fold (fig. C). Note: If the towel already has a casing, skip this step.

6. Right sides together, stitch two 2½"-wide strips together; press open the seam. Repeat until you have at least a 64"-long strip. Right sides together, fold the strip in half lengthwise. Stitch the lengthwise edge and one short end. Turn the tube right side out. Turn in the raw ends on the open short end; stitch.

Use a tube-turning tool or a knitting needle to turn the tube right side out.

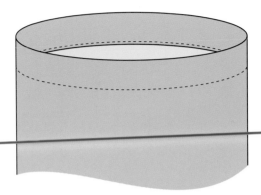

Fig. C
Stitch casing.

7. Thread the fabric strip through the casing; knot each strip end.

**For more storage, create another pocket
and stitch it to the bag back.**

SATCHEL

Designed by Linda Lee

THIS CHARMING CARRYALL EXPANDS to hold everything from gym clothes to office files. Make the straps short for a sporty handbag or long for an over-the-shoulder tote. Find two complementary fabrics, one for the bag and another for the bottom, straps and casing trim, and have some fun making bags for every season.

SUPPLIES

Yardages are based on 44"/45"-wide fabric.

- ½ yard of fabric for bag exterior
- ¾ yard of coordinating fabric for bottom, casing, straps and drawstring
- Safety pin
- Matching all-purpose thread
- Rotary cutter and straight edge
- Chalk marker

CUTTING

From the bag fabric, cut one 17½" x 42" rectangle.

From the coordinating fabric, cut one 2½" x 42" strip for the casing trim, one 8½"-diameter circle for the bottom, four 5½" x 22" rectangles for the straps and two strips 1¼"-wide by the fabric width for the drawstring.

CONSTRUCTING THE SATCHEL

Sew with right sides together and a ½" seam allowance unless otherwise noted.

1. Cut one end of each coordinating 5½" x 22" rectangle to make a point.

2. Sew the 1¼"-wide fabric strips together along the short ends to make one continuous fabric strip that measures 54" long.

3. Fold the 17½" x 42" bag rectangle in half crosswise to make a 17½" x 21" piece; stitch the side seam. Serge- or zigzag-finish the raw edges (fig. A).

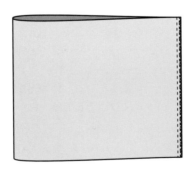

Fig. A
Stitch side seam.

4. Pin one ½" pleat in place along the bag lower edge. Measure and mark 1½" from the edge of the pleat. Fold another ½" pleat at the marking. Repeat around the entire bag lower edge to make approximately 16 pleats. Stitch ½" from the lower edge to hold the pleats in place (fig. B).

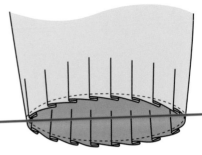

Fig. B
Stitch pleats in place.

5. Clip from the raw edge to the stitching line every ½" along the bag lower edge.

6. Pin the bag to the bottom circle, matching the raw edges and allowing the clipped seam allowance to spread open.

7. Stitch over the previous stitching line to sew the bag to the bottom circle (fig. C).

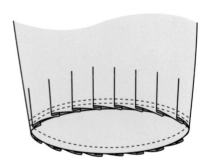

Fig. C
Stitch bag to bottom circle.

tip

For the bottom of the bag to align with the outer circumference of the circle, you may need to clip more often or change the depth of a few pleats.

8. Sew two strap pieces together, leaving the short straight ends open (fig. D). Trim the seam allowances, trim the points, and turn the strap right side out; press. Edgestitch around the strap outer edges; press. Repeat to stitch the two remaining strap pieces.

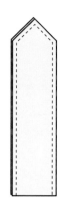

Fig. D
Sew strap pieces together.

tip

It's easier to get crisp, flat edges if you first press the seam allowances over a point presser before turning.

9. Lay the bag flat with the side seam on the right-hand side. Place a pin opposite the seam on the fabric fold on the left-hand side. Refold the bag so the side seam is over the pin mark. Pin-mark the two side folds—these pins mark the center front and center back.

10. Fold each strap in half lengthwise and pin-mark the center of each raw end. Center one strap over the center front and the other over the center back on the wrong side of the bag, aligning the raw edges and pins; baste in place.

11. On the 2½" x 42" casing strip, press ½" to the wrong side of one lengthwise edge. Press ½" to the wrong side of each short end. Starting with one folded end aligned with the side seam, pin the casing strip right side to the bag wrong side, sandwiching the straps and aligning the raw edges. Sew the casing to the bag upper edge (fig. E).

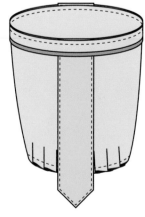

Fig. E
Sew casing to bag.

12. Trim the seam allowance; press open the seam. Turn the casing to the bag right side. Pin the casing in place and edgestitch along the lower edge. The casing remains open at the side seam. Edgestitch along the bag upper edge (fig. F).

Fig. F

13. Wrong sides together, fold the drawstring in half lengthwise; press. Fold each lengthwise raw edge to the center foldline; press. Refold the drawstring on all foldlines and edgestitch along the outer edge, beginning and ending about 2" from each end (fig. G).

Fig. G
Edgestitch drawstring.

14. Attach a safety pin to one drawstring end. Feed the pin and drawstring through one opening of the casing, bringing it out through the opposite opening. Unfold the drawstring ends. Right sides together, sew the short ends together, press open the seam, and refold the drawstring. Complete the edgestitching to make a continuous drawstring.

15. Knot the straps together to complete the handle.

REVERSIBLE PURSE

Designed by Ellen March

HAVE TWICE THE FUN WITH TWO PURSES in one. Turn the purse inside out and vice versa to change the look quickly and easily.

Finished purse size: 12" x 14"

SUPPLIES

- 1 yard each of two 45"-wide coordinating print fabrics
- 2 decorative buttons
- Matching all-purpose thread
- Hand-sewing needle

Source

Fabric.com (www.fabric.com) provided the Amy Butler Belle fabric.

CUTTING

From each of the two coordinating print fabrics, cut two purse pieces using the pattern on page 57 (enlarge the pattern 300%).

CONSTRUCTING THE PURSE

Sew with right sides together and a ½" seam allowances unless otherwise noted.

1. Place one pair of matching purse pieces on a flat work surface with edges and corners aligned. Stitch the purse pieces together along the upper edge; press open the seam. Stitch the side edges independently; press open. Repeat to stitch the second pair of purse sections together. Stitch the lower edges independently, leaving a 5" opening along one lower-edge center for turning (fig. A). Press open the seams.

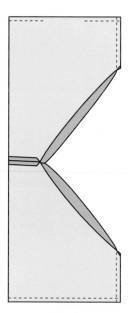

Fig. A
Stitch side then lower edges;
leave opening along one end.

2. With right sides together, place one purse section inside the other, aligning all edges. Pin around the outer edge (fig. B); stitch, and then press open the seam.

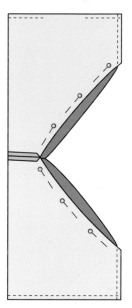

Fig. B
Pin outer edge.

3. Turn the purse right side out through the opening; press.

4. Push one purse section inside the other with wrong sides facing so the opening along one lower edge is exposed. Topstitch the outer edge (fig. C).

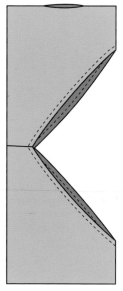

Fig. C

5. Slipstitch the opening closed. Fold the purse along the upper-edge seam and insert the hand-stitched edge into the opposite lower edge (fig. D).

6. Hand stitch each diagonal edge for 5", beginning at the outer-edge corner (fig. E). Catch only the outer fabric in the stitching so it doesn't show through on the reverse side. Stitch a button at the corner. Turn the purse inside out, and repeat to stitch the diagonal edges and corner button.

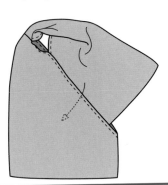

Fig. D
Insert one purse
section into the other.

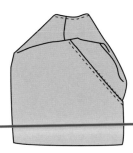

Fig. E
Handstitch diagonal edge.

FABRIC SWAP

From sleek to scampish, there are plenty of ways to personalize your reversible bag.

• For a kid-friendly bag, pair bright cotton prints, and then search your stash or the fabric store for fun novelty buttons.

• Use canvas to create a bag that's perfect for the farmer's market or weekend shopping.

• Choose fabrics and buttons in your school's or favorite team's colors.

• Accessorize flannel with wooden buttons for a homespun look.

• Try different shades of silk for shine or heavy decorator fabrics for texture, and then finish with big faux-jewel buttons.

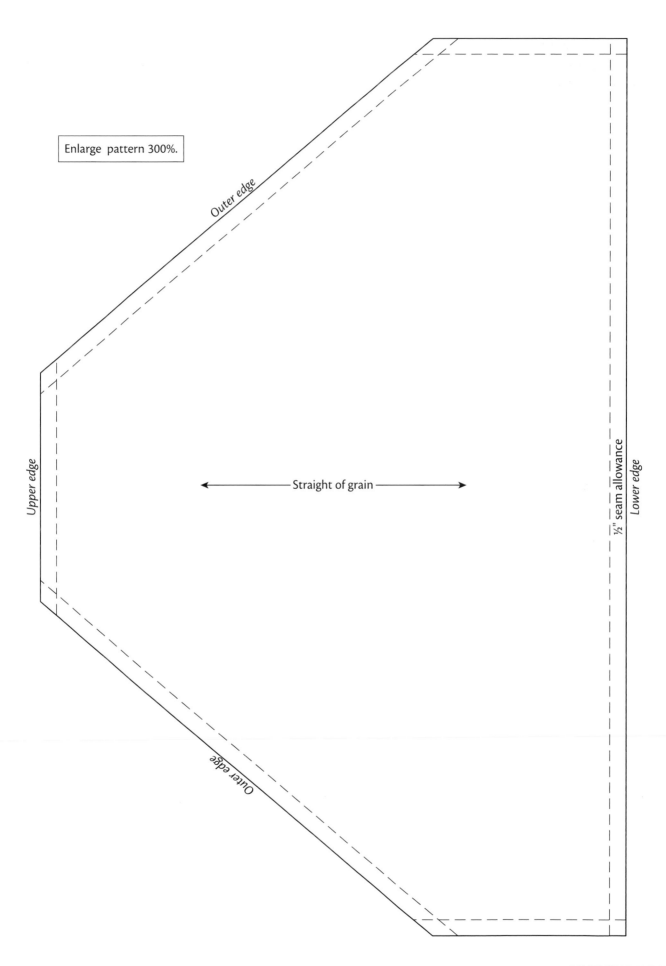

Enlarge pattern 300%.

Outer edge

Upper edge

Straight of grain

½" seam allowance

Lower edge

Outer edge

SIMPLY SASHIKO

Designed by Nancy Shriber

PAIR SASHIKO STITCHING WITH BEAUTIFUL SILK DUPIONI to create a clutch that's the perfect accessory for all your spring events. This little handbag is quick to make, holds a surprising amount of necessities, and takes very little fabric. Plus, the Sashiko stitching is easy and relaxing!

THE SIMPLE BEAUTY OF STAB STITCHING

The word "Sashiko" literally means to stitch or to stab. Sashiko is a humble, simple stitch that originated in Japan. A bit of historical background on this technique reveals that it was a practice of the common people in the early days of cloth restrictions in Japan. The stitch was nothing more than a running stitch that offered a practical and simple method to mend or repair worn areas of hand-woven or homespun cloth.

In addition to simple mending, Sashiko stitching was used to create areas of reinforcement and strength in garments that would receive much wear. For example, the elbow area of a jacket or the knee area of trousers to be worn by a field worker or a fisherman would have additional pieces of cloth stitched and reinforced with Sashiko to create a strong padded section. Despite its utilitarian beginnings, Sashiko is a beautiful way to embellish and enhance a garment, quilt or other project.

Finished handbag size: approximately 14" x 8½"

SUPPLIES

- One 15" square and one 6" square of silk dupioni for bag exterior (fabric A)
- One 15" square of coordinating silk dupioni for lining (fabric B)
- One 15" square of coordinating silk dupioni for binding (fabric C)
- Two 15" squares and one 6" square of cotton flannel or lightweight batting
- Magnetic closure, large snap or set of handbag magnets
- Decorative bead, button, charm or tassel
- Hand sewing needle
- Matching all-purpose thread
- Coordinating embroidery floss, 12-weight cotton thread or decorative machine thread
- Hand embroidery needle
- Sashiko template or quilting grid

MAKING A SAMPLE

Many readily available quilt designs and patterns lend themselves perfectly to Sashiko stitching. However, if you're unfamiliar with the technique and want to test it before locating and purchasing templates, begin by making a small sample.

1. Cut an additional 6" square each from dupioni and flannel.

2. Design a stitching grid on the flannel using a ruler and a pencil or other marking tool. Position the dupioni and fabric squares with wrong sides facing, aligning the outer edges.

3. Thread the hand-sewing needle with three strands of thread. Following the grid lines, stitch the design on the layered squares using a basic running stitch. Remember that you're stitching on the sample wrong side. The thread knot and stitch wrong side are on the flannel or batting side. The stitch will be longer on the dupioni side.

4. After stitching one line, the rhythm of the stitch will become noticeable. The stitches will even out and appear to be about the same length.

5. Once you're comfortable with the technique and want to move forward, check the notions area of a local fabric store or quilt shop for stitching or quilting templates. Templates that offer a design with continuous lines work best for Sashiko projects.

CREATING THE HANDBAG FABRIC

1. Trace the design from the Sashiko template or quilting grid onto one flannel 15" square.

2. Position the fabric A 15" square and marked flannel square with wrong sides together, aligning the outer edges.

3. Thread the hand-sewing needle with three strands of embroidery floss or thread. Knot the thread ends.

4. Stitch over the Sashiko design on the flannel side.

5. Position the fabric B square and remaining flannel 15" square with right sides together. Trim the stitched fabric A/flannel square and the lining/flannel squares to 14" square.

6. If desired, stitch the interior pocket to the lining/flannel square (see "Interior Pocket" on page 61).

7. Position the fabric A/flannel and lining/flannel squares together flannel to flannel, aligning the outer edges. Pin.

8. Cut 2"-wide bias strips from the entire fabric C square. Stitch the strip ends together with right sides facing to create a continuous binding strip.

9. Finish the stacked square by attaching the bias binding strip along the outer edges.

ASSEMBLING THE HANDBAG

1. Position the bound 14" square on a flat work surface. Select one edge as the upper edge.

2. Measure 3" down from the upper edge; fold and press. Measure 5½" up from the lower edge. Fold and press. Unfold the square.

3. Refold the square along the lower foldline to create the bag body. Abut the bag-body side edges.

4. Zigzag stitch each bag-body side, making sure to catch both edges in the stitching (fig. A).

Fig. A

5. Fold the upper corners about 1" toward the bag interior in order to pull the bag body in at an angle. Tack the upper corners in place with a few hand stitches (fig. B).

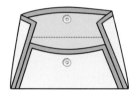

Tack in place.

Fig. B

6. Center the first closure component along the upper-edge center on the lining side. Stitch in place. Center the second component along the bag-body upper edge (fig. C). Stitch in place.

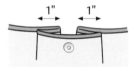

Fig. C

7. Create a soft box pleat at the bag-body center front by folding the upper edge 1" toward the closure (fig. D).

1"   1"

Fig. D

8. Stitch in the ditch below the bias binding on the bag-body upper edge to secure the pleat. Stitch the decorative charm or bead at the upper-edge center on the doupioni side. If desired, add additional charms, tassels, decorative buttons or beads to embellish the bag.

STRESS-FREE CLOSURE

If you're using a magnetic closure, insert the closure legs into a sturdy, nonraveling-type fabric rather than directly into the dupioni. Measure the closure back plate. Cut four nonraveling fabric squares that are approximately ¼" larger than the plate. Center and push the legs through one fabric square. Position the second piece of fabric behind the back plate. Stitch to the bag upper-edge lining side. Repeat for the second closure component, stitching it to the bag-body upper edge.

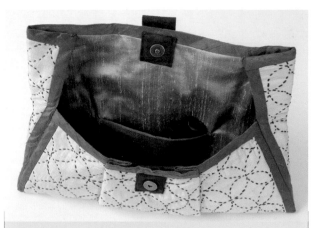

INTERIOR POCKET

1. Position the fabric A and flannel 6" squares with wrong sides together. Fold the paired squares in half, flannel side out.

2. Stitch around the perimeter using a ¼" seam allowance, leaving a small opening along one long side for turning. Turn the pocket right side out; press. Hand stitch the opening closed.

3. Position the pocket on the lining/flannel square, centered between the upper and lower folds. Pin.

4. Stitch around the pocket side and lower edges.

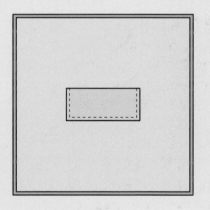

ASIAN PURSE–UASION

Designed by Pamela K. Archer

THESE UNIQUE, ASIAN-INSPIRED BAGS sew up in just a few hours. Better make two—one to give and another for yourself!

Choose any Asian-themed fabric in a printed or woven design. Accents of black paired with vibrant colors, in patterns of dragons, flowers, dragonflies and Chinese characters, are a standard for oriental fabrics. Consider cotton prints, silk brocades or even home-dec fabrics and trims. Solid fabrics like sueded rayon or silk dupioni provide a background to play up appliqués cut from the Asian-themed print. Don't be limited by thinking you must match the background fabric with the appliqué main color. Try using another color from the main motif—the contrast can be pleasantly surprising and provides extra pop you won't find in a basic matching color.

Once you've decided on the fabric, add a personal touch with appliqués and embellishments, and then add unique beaded handle accents.

From left to right: Gold Oriental Bag, Black Chinese Bag, Blue Japanese Bag.

BLUE JAPANESE OR GOLD ORIENTAL BAG

Finished Blue Japanese Bag size:
    8½" x 10" (excluding straps)

Finished Gold Oriental Bag size:
    7" x 8" (excluding straps)

SUPPLIES

Yardages are based on 44"/45"-wide fabric.

For each bag:
- ¾ yard of print fabric for motifs, lining and optional piping
- ⅓ yard of coordinating solid fabric for bag exterior
- ⅙ yard of black fabric for upper band and zipper panel
- 2⅔ yards of black ⅜" cording
- ⅙ yard of lightweight fusible interfacing
- ¼ yard of paper-backed fusible web
- Topstitching needle
- Black rayon embroidery thread
- All-purpose thread: color to match solid fabric and black

For blue bag:
- ⅓ yard of heavyweight sew-in interfacing
- Black 7" zipper

For gold bag:
- ⅓ yard of heavyweight fusible fleece
- ⅛ yard of lightweight fusible interfacing
- Black 5" zipper
- Turquoise topstitching thread
- Turquoise seed beads

tip

Fusible fleece provides firm body to an otherwise soft fabric.

CUTTING

Dimensions given first are for the Blue Japanese Bag, with dimensions for the Gold Oriental Bag in parentheses.

From the solid fabric, cut two 9" x 10" (8" x 9") rectangles for the bag body and two 10" x 11" (8" x 9") rectangles for the lining.

From the sew-in interfacing (fusible fleece), cut two 9" x 10" (8" x 9") rectangles for the bag body and two 3" x 9½" (3½" x 8") rectangles for the upper band.

From the black fabric, cut two zipper panels, 2" wide and the length of the zipper tape.

From the print fabric, cut two 1½" x 8¾" bias strips for the piping (optional).

PREPARING THE BAG PIECES

1. For the blue bag, measure ¼" in from each short side (9" edge) of the solid-color fabric and interfacing bag body rectangles and make a mark. Draw a line connecting the marks to the lower corners (fig. A); cut along the line.

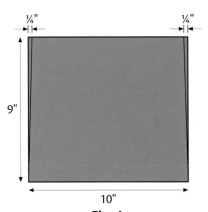

Fig. A
Taper bag bodies to lower corners.

2. For the blue bag, machine baste the interfacing to the wrong side of each bag body and band piece, stitching ⅜" from all edges. Trim the excess interfacing close to the stitching.

   For the gold bag, trim ⅜" from the edge of each fusible fleece piece. Following the manufacturer's instructions, fuse the fleece to the wrong side of the corresponding bag body and band pieces.

3. Select two or more motifs from the print fabric to use as appliqués. Motifs can be different on opposite bag sides. Following the manufacturer's instructions, apply paper-backed fusible web to each motif wrong side. Trim around the motifs, leaving an extra ½" all around.

Position the selected motif(s) on the right side of each bag body piece. (For the gold bag, when placing motifs, keep in mind that the 8" rectangle edge is the upper edge and the bag band will cover the upper third of the bag. The construction of the gold bag is slightly different from the blue bag because it uses fusible fleece. Fusing one large piece of fleece to the entire bag and then adding the band overlay prevents a ridge caused by a seam in the fleece.) Once you're pleased with the placement, do a final trimming ⅛" beyond the desired motif. Peel off the paper backing and fuse the motif to the bag bodies. Trimming twice ensures that you'll have a clean edge after handling the appliqués to test the placement.

4. Set the machine for a satin stitch (3.5 mm wide, 0.2 mm long) and thread the needle with black rayon embroidery thread. Sew along the motif edges. To avoid bulk in the seam allowances, don't satin stitch edges that will be caught in seams.

5. For the blue bag, at each end of the piping strips, fold under ½" and press. Fold the strip in half lengthwise with wrong sides together and press again. Aligning the long raw edges, baste the piping to the side seams of one bag body. Begin the piping ¾" from the bag lower edge and end ½" from the upper edge.

For the gold bag, using turquoise topstitching thread, outline a few of the motif's design elements with straight stitching. Hand stitch turquoise seed beads to the outlined elements, placing one bead about every ¼" to highlight an important motif. Coordinating seed beads can be stitched to the bag's surface to add dimension, texture and emphasis.

Hand stitch seed beads to highlight motifs.

CONSTRUCTING THE BAG

Sew with right sides together and a ½" seam allowance unless otherwise noted.

1. For the blue bag, sew the shorter (upper) edge of each bag body to a band lengthwise edge. Be careful not to catch the piping in the stitching.

For the gold bag, place the band 2½" from the bag shorter (upper) edge; stitch 3" from the bag upper edge. Press the band toward the bag upper edge, and baste the bag and band raw edges together (fig. B).

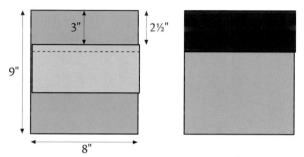

Fig. B
Stitch band to bag body; press band up and baste.

2. Pin the bag bodies together along the long edges (side seams), matching the band/body seams. Stitch the side seams, ending ½" from the lower edges, and press open.

3. Stitch the bag bodies together along the lower edges, beginning and ending ½" from the sides; press open. Box the bag corners. Right sides together, align the lower edge with the adjoining side seam to form a point. Draw a line ½" from the point; stitch across the point to form a triangle (fig. C). For a thicker bag, increase the depth of this seam. Repeat for the remaining lower bag corner. Trim the corners and turn the bag right side out.

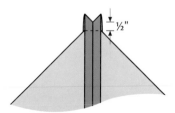

Fig. C
Align bottom and side seams, and box corners.

4. Construct the lining using the same method as for the bag body, except leave a 4" opening in the lower seam for turning the bag right side out.

5. On the upper edge of the band/bag only, make a ½" clip into the seam allowance ⅝" on either side of each side seam.

6. Cut the cording into two equal pieces; fold each piece in half again and cut the fold. With a doubled cord, tie a knot 3" from each end. Repeat for the other doubled cord.

To prevent fraying, wrap tape around the cording before cutting. After the cording is securely stitched in position, remove the tape and apply seam sealant to the ends.

7. Position a handle on the right side of the bag at the upper edge. Aligning the raw edges of the bag and cording, place each handle end 2" (1¾") from the bag side seam. Baste in place (fig. D). Repeat to baste the remaining handle to the other bag side. Adjust the handles as needed so they're the same length.

Fig. D
Baste handle to bag upper edge.

BEADAZZLED BAGS

The bag handles are adorned with an assortment of wood, clay and metal beads threaded onto rattail cord and secured in the handle knot. Check your local craft store, garage sales or your jewelry box for some colorful, unique beads. Be sure the beads have a hole large enough to accommodate one or two cord thicknesses.

Line up the beads on a flat surface, and arrange them until you're satisfied with the effect.

To create the beaded tassel end, either thread both ends of 12" of rattail cord through one large bead or Chinese coin, and then bring the thread loops back through the loop (as shown below), or thread a single cord end through a large bead and center the bead.

Thread the cord ends through more beads, threading both ends through large beads and separating the ends for smaller beads.

Loosen one knot in the bag handle, and tie the tassel ends in a knot around the cord. Tighten the handle knot, hiding the tassel ends.

8. Fold each zipper panel rectangle in half lengthwise with wrong sides together; press. Pin each rectangle folded edge close to the zipper teeth, and stitch next to the fold with a zipper foot (fig. E). Unzip the zipper.

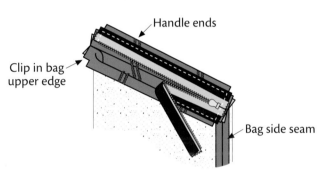

Fig. E
Stitch folded rectangles
to zipper tape.

9. Aligning the long raw edges, baste each side of the zipper panel to the bag upper edge between the clips, sandwiching the handle ends.

10. On the narrow sides of the bag, baste the zipper panel short ends to the bag from clip to clip, matching the bag side seam with the zipper opening (fig. F). Trim any excess zipper panel. *Don't turn the zipper to the finished position.*

Handle ends

Clip in bag
upper edge

Bag side seam

Fig. F
Baste zipper panel to bag body.

FINISHING

1. Slip the lining, right side out, into the bag, which is still wrong side out, sandwiching the handles and zipper panel, and aligning the raw edges and side seams. Stitch the bag to the lining around the upper edge. Trim the seam allowances to ¼", and clip the corners.

2. Turn the bag right side out through the opening in the lining. Slipstitch the opening closed and tuck the lining into the bag. Hand tack the lining to the bag at the lower corners.

BLACK CHINESE BAG

Finished size: 10" x 10" (excluding straps)

Supplies
Yardages are based on 44"/45"-wide fabric.

• ⅓ yard of Asian-print fabric for bag exterior

• ⅛ yard of black fabric for bag exterior

• 1 yard of contrast fabric for piping and lining

• 5⅓ yards of ½" cotton filler cord

• 1½ yards of ¼" cotton filler cord

• ⅓ yard of heavyweight sew-in interfacing

• 7" zipper

• Matching all-purpose thread

This Black Chinese Bag variation has piped seams, plus filled cording for the handles.

CUTTING

From the contrast fabric, cut two 1½" x 30" bias strips for the piping along the bag seams, and two 2½" x 48" bias strips for the corded handles. From the remaining contrast fabric, cut two 11" squares for the lining.

From the Asian-print fabric, cut two 11"-square bag bodies, centering the desired motif. Cut two 11" squares from sew-in interfacing.

From the black fabric, cut two zipper panels, 2" wide and the length of the zipper tape.

CONSTRUCTING THE BAG

Sew with right sides together and a ½" seam allowance unless otherwise noted.

1. Machine baste the interfacing to the wrong side of each bag body, stitching ⅜" from all edges. Trim the interfacing close to the stitching.

2. Fold each 1½" bias strip, wrong sides together, over ¼" filler cord. With a zipper foot, sew close to the cord. Cut the piping into the following: one 9½" piece, two 10" pieces and two 11" pieces. On each piping end, remove a few stitches and trim the cord ½" from the fabric strip end so the seam allowances won't be bulky.

3. With raw edges even, baste the piping to the bag body in the following order. Use a zipper foot and stitch as close to the cord as possible. On each bag-body upper edge, baste 11" of piping. Center the 9½" piping along the lower edge of one bag body and baste. On the same bag body, baste a 10" length of piping on each side seam, beginning the piping ¾" from the bag lower edge.

4. Cut the ½" filler cord in half. Beginning at one cord end, fold a 2½"-wide bias strip right sides together around the cord. Machine baste across the strip end in the middle of the cord. Using a zipper foot and a short stitch length, sew close to the cord without catching it in the stitching (fig. G). Trim the seam allowances to ¼".

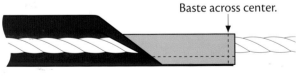

Fig. G
Fold bias strip around cord and stitch.

5. Turn each handle right side out by pulling the stitched fabric over the excess cord length. Remove the basting at the end of the handle and trim the remaining cord. Repeat to make the second handle piece.

6. Cut each handle piece in half. At each end, slide back the fabric and clip the cord ½" from the handle end. Construct the double-corded handles and baste them to the bag as for the Blue Japanese Bag.

7. Using a zipper foot to stitch close to the piping, sew the bag bodies together as described on page 65 for the Blue Japanese Bag, but do not clip the bag upper edge. Fold the seam allowances under at the bag upper edge, pressing the piping toward the bag upper edge.

8. Construct the lining as described for the Blue Japanese Bag. On the upper edge of the lining, make a ½" clip into the seam allowance ⅝" on either side of each side seam. Fold the lining upper edge under ½" and press.

9. Construct the zipper panel as described for the Blue Japanese Bag. With the lining wrong side out and the zipper right side up, align the long raw edges of the zipper panel with the lining upper edge; baste between the clips.

10. On the narrow sides of the bag, baste the zipper panel short ends to the lining from clip to clip, matching the lining side seam with the zipper opening. This step is similar to that shown in figure F on page 67, except the zipper panel will be face up.

11. Trim across the corners, and press the seam allowances toward the lining. Unzip the zipper, and slip the lining into the bag with wrong sides together.

12. Pin the bag to the zipper panel with the piping seamline along the lining/zipper panel seamline. Using a zipper foot, stitch in the ditch just under the piping from the right side (fig. H).

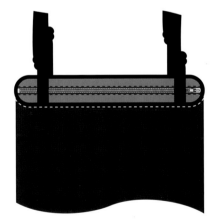

Fig. H
Stitch in the ditch below piping.

13. Complete the bag according to the Blue Japanese Bag instructions.

BANGLE BAG

Designed by Lisa Shepard Stewart

THIS PROJECT IS LIKE TWO ACCESSORIES IN ONE. The
handles are bracelets, so you can wear the bag on your wrist
and keep your hands free. So find a pair of bangles you love,
find fabric to match, and start stitching.

tip

To give the featured bag cultural style, use the following fabrics or similar in style.
Main fabric: Bogolan mudcloth
Lining fabric: African cotton fabric

MAIN FABRIC

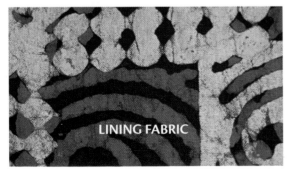

LINING FABRIC

CUTTING

From the main fabric, cut one 10" x 15" rectangle for the body and two 3½" squares for the tabs.

From the interfacing, cut two 3½" squares.

CONSTRUCTING THE BAG

Sew with right sides together and a ½" seam allowance unless otherwise noted.

1. Fuse an interfacing square to the wrong side of each main fabric square following the manufacturer's instructions. Fold opposite tab edges toward the interfacing side so they overlap and the tab measures 1½" wide (fig. A). Secure with hand or machine stitching, fabric glue or fusible tape. Repeat to create the second tab.

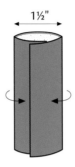

1½"

Fig. A
Fold in tab edges.

2. Wrap one tab around each bangle with the seam facing the inside. Using a zipper foot, stitch through both layers of the tab ¼" from the bangle outer edge. Trim the tab ends to ¼" (fig. B).

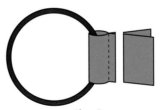

Fig. B
Stitch tab; trim ends.

3. Pin-mark the center of the bag upper edge and ½" from each side. Center the tabs between the pins, aligning the raw edges; baste (fig. C).

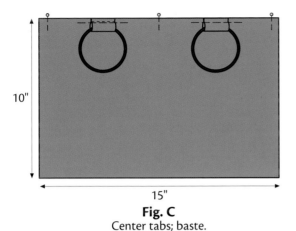

Fig. C
Center tabs; baste.

4. Turn under ¼" toward the wrong side on each 10" edge of the lining rectangle; press. Right sides together, pin the lining and main-fabric rectangle together along the upper edge. Stitch, beginning and ending ½" from each side. Use a zipper foot to stitch close to the bangles. Open the seam; press the seam toward the lining. Understitch the seam through both the lining and the seam allowance, leaving ½" unstitched at each side edge; press (fig. D). Understitching prevents the lining from rolling over the bag upper edge.

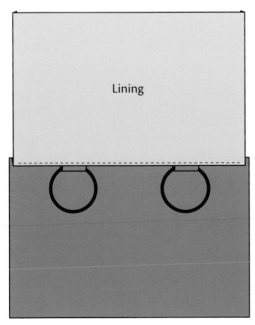

Fig. D
Understitch lining.

5. Pin the main-fabric and lining rectangles together along the lower edge. Stitch, beginning and ending ½" from each side edge. Turn the bag right side out; press. Pin only the main fabrics together at the side edge; stitch (fig. E). Press open the seam, using steam to flatten the bulk. Align the lining pressed edges to conceal the main side seam, slightly overlapping the lining edges. Hand stitch the lining using small close stitches. Turn the bag right side out.

Fig. E
Stitch side seam.

6. With the lining right sides together, pin the bag lower edge. Stitch through all layers using a ¼" seam, carefully reinforcing the stitching through the bulk of the corners.

7. Reinforce the stitching across the bag upper edge at the tabs about ¼" from the bag edge (fig. F).

Fig. F
Reinforce stitching.

8. Optional: Attach magnetic snap closures to the inside of the bag, just below the bangle tabs.

BUTTON BOUQUET PURSE

Designed by Linda Lee

EVEN IN THE MIDDLE OF WINTER, this pretty posie-adorned purse will remind you of sunnier days to come. Use up buttons, trim and fabric from other sewing projects to create a cute portable garden.

Finished size: 7" x 5½" (excluding straps)

SUPPLIES

Yardages are based on 44"/45"-wide fabric.

- ¼ yard of medium- to heavyweight fabric for bag exterior
- ¼ yard of fabric for lining
- 7" zipper
- 1 package of extra-wide double-fold bias tape
- ¼ yard each of 6 assorted ribbons, rickrack or other trims
- 6 to 9 assorted buttons
- 5 small scraps of faux suede, vinyl or other nonraveling fabric
- Matching and contrasting all-purpose thread
- Fusible-web tape
- Pinking shears

Stack the flower-center buttons for more dimension.

CUTTING

From both the main fabric and the lining fabric, cut two 6½" x 8" rectangles.

From the bias tape, cut one 51" length.

From the scraps of nonraveling fabrics, use pinking shears to cut five circles of various sizes ranging from 1" to 1½" in diameter.

CONSTRUCTING THE PURSE

Sew with right sides together and a ½" seam allowance unless otherwise noted.

1. Position one main fabric rectangle right side up on a flat work surface, choosing one long edge as the upper edge. Referring to the photo for inspiration, decorate the rectangle. Use the faux suede circles for the flowers, the assorted trims for the flower stems, and the buttons for the flower centers. Once you're happy with the design, attach the circles and trim strips with fusible-web tape following the manufacturer's instructions. Stitch down the center of each trim strip. Stitch the buttons in place at the circle centers.

2. Position the zipper right side down over the decorated fabric rectangle right side, aligning the zipper tape upper edge with the fabric upper edge (fig. A). Use fusible-web tape to hold the zipper tape upper side in place.

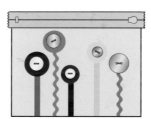

Fig. A
Position zipper along upper edge.

3. Position one lining rectangle over the decorated rectangle, sandwiching the zipper in between. Using your zipper foot, stitch ¼" from the upper edge through all three layers (fig. B).

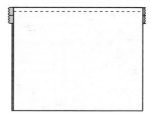

Fig. B
Stitch ¼" from upper edge.

4. Unfold the lining and main fabric rectangles, allowing the zipper to flip upward and the seam allowance to fold downward behind the decorated rectangle upper edge. Stitch along the folded edge next to the zipper teeth, stitching through the bag piece, the zipper tape and the seam allowance (fig. C).

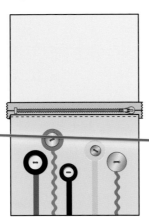

Fig. C
Stitch along folded edge.

5. Repeat steps 2–4 to attach the remaining main fabric and lining rectangles to the remaining zipper side.

6. Open the zipper. Stitch around the bag and lining outer perimeter in a continuous stitching line, leaving a 4" opening along the lining long edge for turning (fig. D). Trim off the excess zipper tape and then clip the main fabric and lining corners.

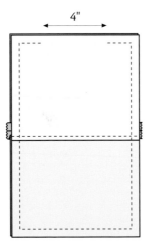

Fig. D
Stitch, leaving opening for turning.

7. Set the machine for a zigzag stitch. Using your regular sewing machine foot, with the bias tape still folded, stitch lengthwise down the tape center.

8. Measure down 1½" from the main fabric rectangle upper edge along each side seam. Pin one bias tape end at each mark. Drop the sewing machine feed dogs. Zigzag stitch the ends in place.

9. Turn the bag right side out through the lining opening. Turn the lining lower edge seam allowances to the inside and edgestitch the opening closed. Insert the lining into the bag. Carefully press the lining to the bag inside along the zipper opening.

10. Stitch a button over each strap raw end (fig. E).

Fig. E
Stitch buttons over strap ends.

Hide the strap ends with a cute coordinating button.

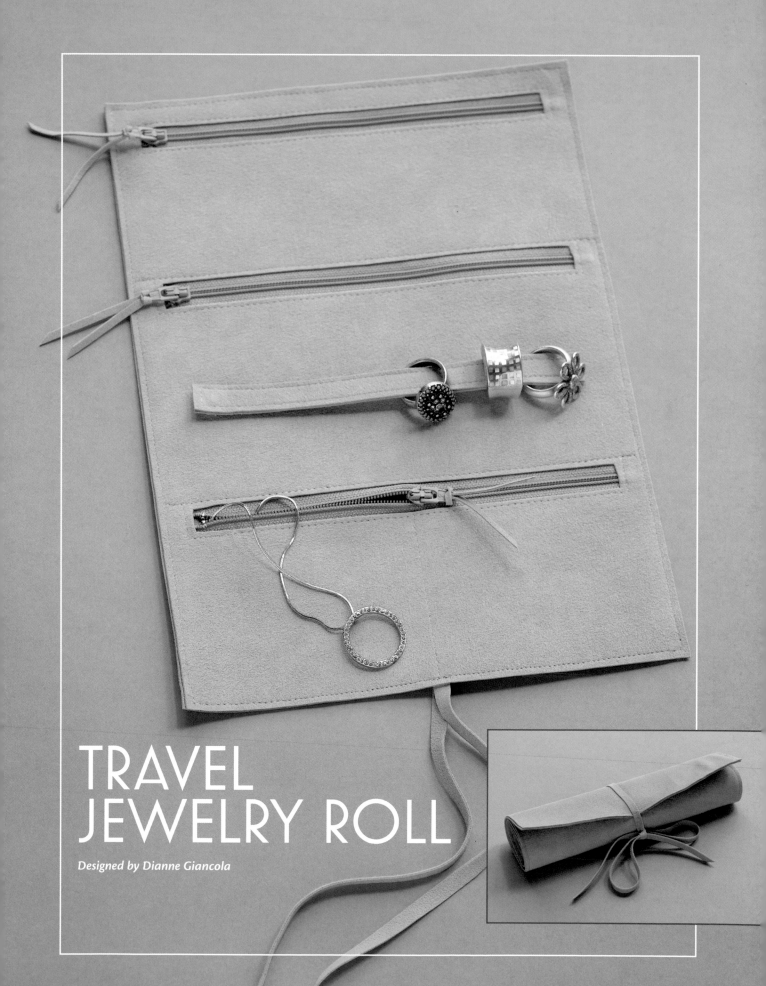

TRAVEL
JEWELRY ROLL

Designed by Dianne Giancola

GETTING READY TO TAKE A TRIP?

Make a travel-friendly faux suede jewelry roll to hold rings, bracelets and necklaces. Sewing on faux suede is simple if you keep a few tips in mind. Instead of pins, use a fabric glue stick, double-sided tape or general household transparent tape to baste fabric layers together. Suede doesn't ravel, so there's no need to finish the raw edges.

Finished jewelry roll size: 8" x 11" (flat)

SUPPLIES

• ½ yard of 45"-wide mediumweight faux suede fabric (such as Ultrasuede)

• Three 7" to 9" contrasting zippers

• Matching all-purpose thread

• One ⅜" silver snap

• Fabric-marking pen

• Rotary cutter and mat

• Double-sided ¼" basting tape (such as Collins Wash-A-Way Wonder Tape)

• Fabric glue stick (such as Collins Fabric Glue Stick)

• Transparent household tape

Sources

Hartsdale Fabrics (www.hartsdalefabrics.com, 914-428-7780) was the source of the chartreuse Ultrasuede.

Prym Consumer USA (www.dritz.com) provided the Collins Fabric Glue Stick and the Wash-A-Way Wonder Tape.

For more information about Ultrasuede fabric, visit www.ultrasuede.com.

CUTTING

Faux suede sometimes appears lighter on one side. Choose one fabric side as the right side; mark the wrong side with a piece of tape. Use the rotary cutter, mat and ruler to cut straight, clean edges.

From the faux suede, cut two 8" x 11" rectangles for the body, two ½" x 6½" strips for the ring holder, one ¼" x 22" strip for the tie and three ⅛" x 6" strips for the zipper pulls.

CONSTRUCTING THE JEWELRY ROLL

1. Position one 8" x 11" body rectangle on the cutting mat with one short edge as the lower edge. Draw three ⅜" x 7" zipper slot openings. The upper opening is ½" from the upper and side edges. The center opening is 3½" from the upper edge and ½" from the side edges. The lower opening is 7½" from the upper edge and ½" from the side edges. Cut out each opening (fig. A).

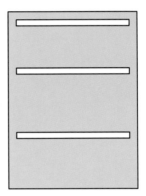

Fig. A
Cut out each opening.

2. To create the ring holder, lightly dab the fabric glue stick on one ½" x 6½" strip. Finger-press it to the other ½" x 6½" strip, aligning all edges. Allow the glue to dry for a few minutes. Stitch around the strip perimeter ⅛" from the outer edges.

Use a slightly longer stitch length and a size 14 needle when sewing on faux suede. If skipped stitches occur, try using a needle appropriate for stretch fabrics.

When topstitching, always begin on a side edge, never at a corner. Overlap the stitching slightly at the beginning and end.

3. Position the stitched strip on the 8" x 11" rectangle, centering it lengthwise between the center and lower zipper openings. Tape in place (fig. B). Stitch widthwise across the strip about ⅛" from the short right-hand end.

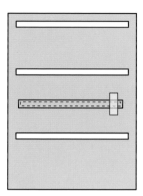

Fig. B
Tape strip in place.

4. Hand sew the snap ball to the strip left short end, about ⅛" from the edge. Hand sew the socket in place to the suede rectangle (fig. C).

Fig. C
Hand sew socket in place.

5. Apply the double-sided basting tape to one zipper right side close to the long edges; peel away the paper. Position the zipper right side up on a flat surface with the tab pulled closed to the left. Right side up, center the rectangle upper opening over the zipper; finger-press in place (fig. D). Using a zipper foot, stitch around the opening perimeter close to the cut edges. Trim the zipper ends close to the opening. Remove the basting tape. Repeat for the remaining zippers.

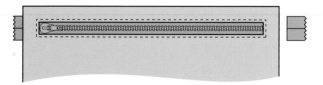

Fig. D
Center rectangle upper opening
over zipper; finger-press.

6. Position the remaining 8" x 11" rectangle wrong side up. Lightly dab the glue stick around the outer edges. Place the first rectangle right side up over the second rectangle,

aligning the outer edges; finger-press. Stitch the rectangle perimeter close to the edge through both fabric layers.

7. To create the upper necklace pocket, stitch widthwise across the rectangle along the center zipper opening upper edge; backstitch at each end.

8. To create the two lower pockets, stitch widthwise across the rectangle along the lower zipper opening upper edge; backstitch at each end. Mark the rectangle center along the lower edge. Stitch from the mark to the lower zipper opening lower edge; backstitch (fig. E).

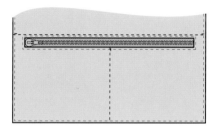

Fig. E
Stitch from mark to lower zipper
opening lower edge; backstitch.

9. Fold the ¼" x 22" strip widthwise so one end extends about 1" past the other. Position the fold on the outer rectangle lower edge center. Stitch back and forth across the fold a few times (fig. F).

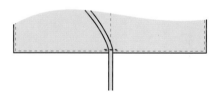

Fig. F
Stitch back and forth across fold.

10. Trim the short ends of one ⅛" x 6" strip at an angle. Insert the trimmed ends one at a time through one zipper pull hole. Even out the strip tails, insert them into the strip loop, and pull to secure. Trim the tails diagonally so that they're each about 1½" long (fig. G). Repeat for the other two zippers.

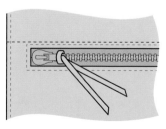

Fig. G
Trim tails diagonally to 1½" long.

HAVE WINE, WILL TRAVEL

Designed by Linda Turner Griepentrog

TOTING WINE OR SPARKLING BEVERAGES
to a friend's party or outdoor picnic is risk free
with this handy, insulated carrier that keeps two
bottles protected and cold for hours.

Finished size: 11" x 17"

SUPPLIES

- ½ yard of 45"-wide double-sided neoprene fabric
- 1½ yards of ¼"-wide fold-over elastic
- Size 90/14 Microtex needle

Sources

Find neoprene fabrics at:

- Denver Fabrics (www.denverfabrics.com, 800-468-0602).
- Rose City Textiles (RCT Fabrics) (www.rctfabrics.com, 503-229-0395).
- Seattle Fabrics (www.seattlefabrics.com, 866-925-0670).

CUTTING

From the neoprene, cut one tote piece, using the pattern on page 80 (enlarge the pattern 200%).

CONSTRUCTING THE TOTE

1. Bind the hand holes and curved upper edges with fold-over elastic. Fold the elastic over the fabric edge, placing the widest portion of the elastic on the wrong side and aligning the indentation with the raw edge. Set the machine for a narrow, short zigzag (2 mm long, 2.5 mm wide) and stitch from the right side, catching all layers and stretching the binding slightly while sewing. To join, abut the elastic ends and stitch across the width to secure (fig. A).

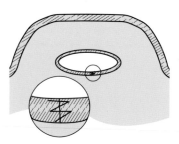

Fig. A
Abut elastic ends; stitch.

2. Fold the tote in half lengthwise with right sides together. Stitch the side and lower edges with a ¼" seam allowance. Turn right side out.

3. Flatten the tote and pin the side and lower seams flat. Chalk-mark a center line beginning 3" below the hand hole and ending 2" above the lower seam. Stitch three parallel lines to create the center divider—one on the chalk line and the others ¼" on either side; backstitch at each end to secure (fig. B).

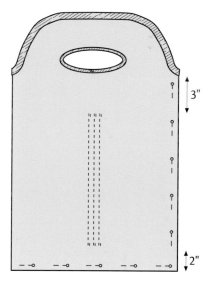

Fig. B
Pin side and lower seams flat;
stitch divider lines.

WORKING WITH NEOPRENE

Neoprene is a dense, synthetic rubber material with fabric on one or both sides. It's commonly used for mouse pads, computer cases and beverage coolers. Take the fear out of sewing neoprene by following these simple tips:

- Stitch the seams with a long, narrow zigzag to maintain the fabric's inherent stretch.
- Use a 90/14 Microtex needle and polyester or nylon thread.
- Do not iron. Finger-press the seams and use topstitching to secure them if needed.

tip

Tack an elastic loop to the tote's upper side seam to hold a corkscrew.

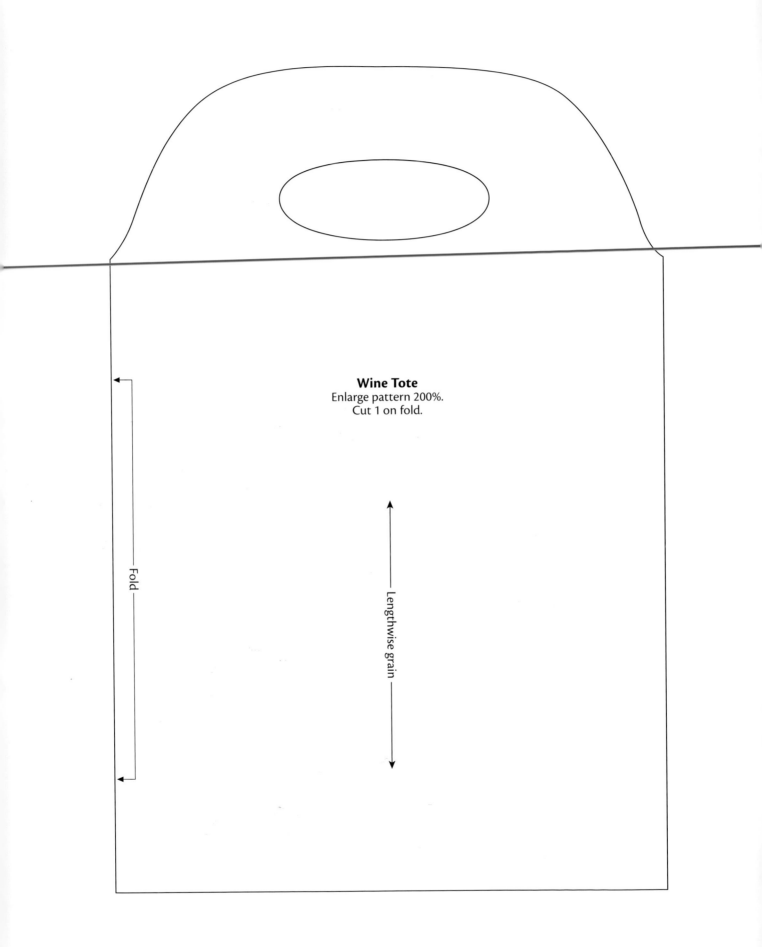

Wine Tote
Enlarge pattern 200%.
Cut 1 on fold.

Fold

Lengthwise grain

CORDUROY PURSE

Designed by Ellen March

THIS BASIC PURSE will give your sewing confidence a boost. Choose three coordinating corduroy fabrics for the body and a funky fabric for the lining. Constructing this hip accessory is so easy you can make one for each of your friends in no time. Their fall wardrobes will thank you.

SUPPLIES

Yardages are based on 44"/45"-wide fabric.

- ⅓ yard each of 2 coordinating corduroy fabrics for body/flap and front (fabrics A & B)
- ⅔ yard of coordinating corduroy fabric for strap
- ⅓ yard of cotton fabric for lining
- Matching all-purpose thread

tip

For a "green" version, recycle old pairs of corduroy pants from your closet or a thrift store instead of buying fabric.

CUTTING

Enlarging 125%, make one copy each of the purse body/flap and front patterns on pages 84 and 85 and use them to cut the purse pieces.

From the body/flap fabric (fabric A), cut one purse body/flap.

From the purse front fabric (fabric B), cut one purse front.

From the cotton lining fabric, cut one purse body/flap and one purse front.

From the strap fabric, cut four 4¾" x 18¾" rectangles.

CONSTRUCTING THE PURSE

Sew with right sides together and a ½" seam allowance unless otherwise noted.

1. Place two strap rectangles together and stitch along one short end. Zigzag-finish the seam and press it open. Stitch and press the remaining strap rectangles in the same manner. Place the two resulting straps right sides together. Stitch along one short end. Zigzag-finish the seam and press open.

2. Press under one strap short end ¼" to the wrong side. Fold the strap in half lengthwise. Stitch the long raw edge; press open the seam. Turn the fabric tube right side out. Press the seam to the strap center. Insert the strap raw end ½" into the folded end, aligning the seamlines and making sure the strap isn't twisted. Stitch close to the fold through all layers. Stitch again ¼" from the first stitching (fig. A).

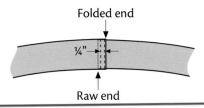

Folded end

¼"

Raw end

Fig. A

3. Stitch the fabric A and lining body/flap pieces together, leaving a 3" opening along the lower edge for turning. Turn the purse body/flap right side out. Fold the opening allowance ¼" toward the wrong side to temporarily close the opening; press the purse perimeter (fig. B).

¼"

3"

Fig. B
Turn purse body right side out; press.

4. Stitch the fabric B and lining purse fronts together, leaving a 3" opening along the lower edge for turning. Turn the purse front right side out. Temporarily close the opening as directed in step 3; press.

5. Fold the purse body/flap in half lengthwise to find the center. Pin-mark the lower edge center. Repeat to pin-mark the lower edge center of the purse front.

6. Align the strap stitching line that's closer to the fold with the purse body/flap lower edge center; pin. Make sure the seamline is facing you, not the purse body/flap. Continue pinning the strap to the purse body/flap up to the flap foldline (fig. C). Stitch the strap to the purse body/flap using a ⅛" seam, removing the pins as you sew and closing the opening with the stitches.

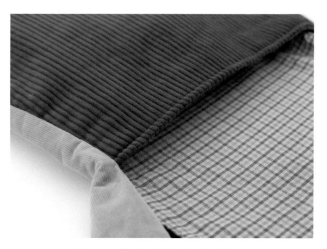

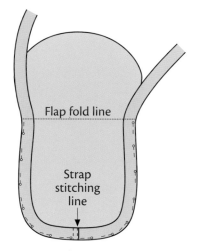

Fig. C
Pin strap to purse body/flap.

7. Place the purse front over the purse body/flap, aligning the lower edge centers. Pin the opposite strap long edge to the purse front. Stitch the strap to the purse front using a ⅛" seam; backstitch at both purse front upper edges.

Choose a funky fabric for the lining.

8. Turn the purse right side out. Topstitch the flap edge (fig. D).

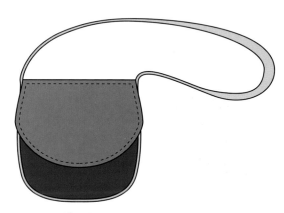

Fig. D
Topstitch flap edge.

ADD SOME BLING
A button, brooch or decorative tassel changes the look of the purse to reflect your personal style.

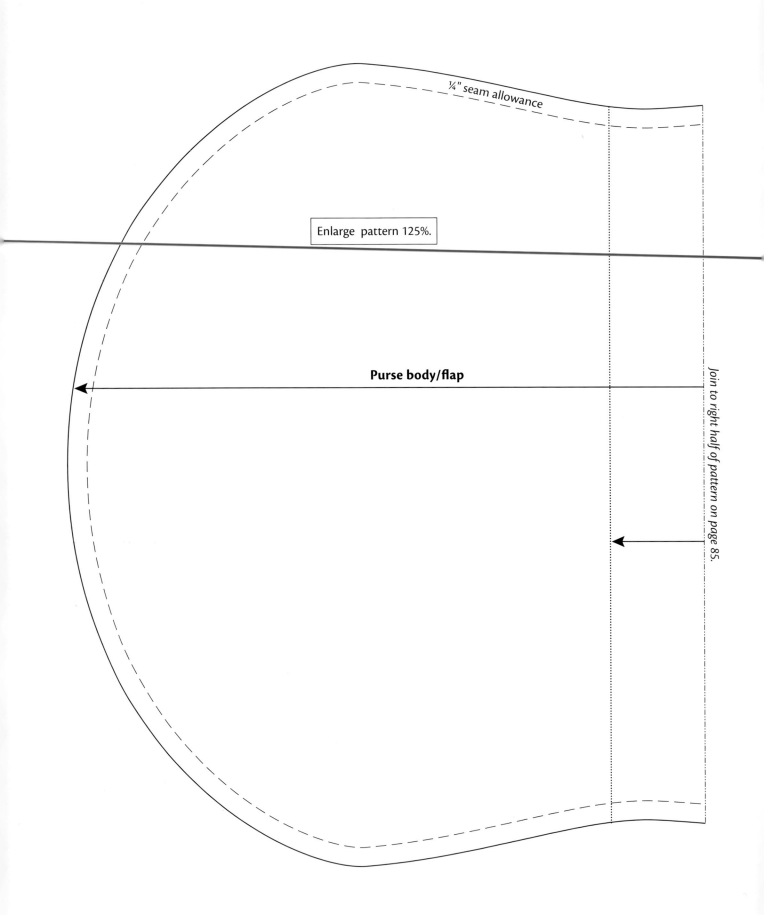

¼" seam allowance

Enlarge pattern 125%.

Purse body/flap

Join to right half of pattern on page 85.

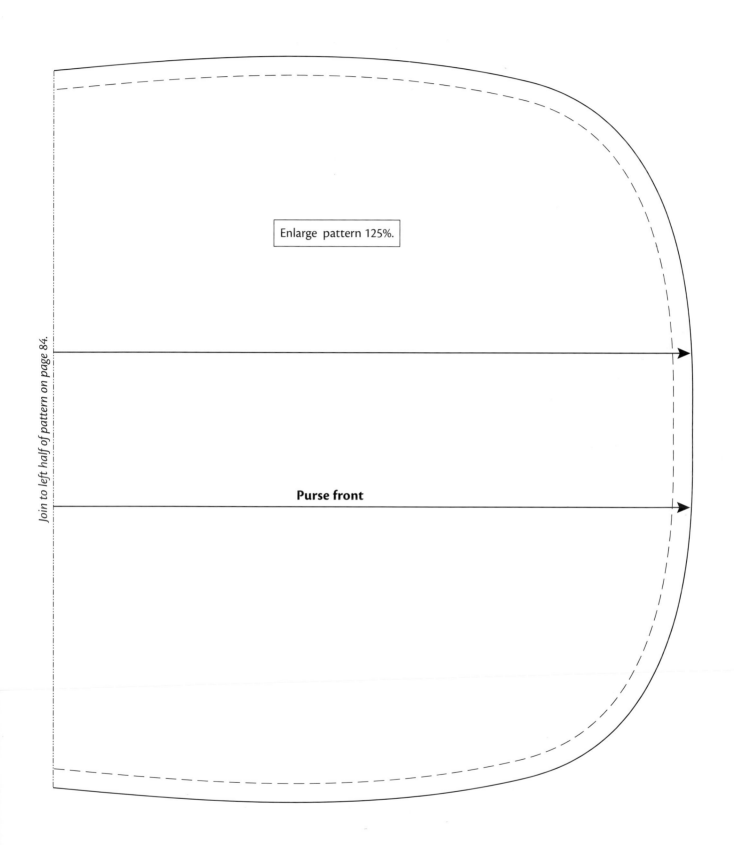

Enlarge pattern 125%.

Join to left half of pattern on page 84.

Purse front

MAD FOR PLAID

Designed by Pamela K. Archer

A CLASSIC WOOL TOTE makes a perfect gift for a gal on the go. Complete with metal feet, a durable lining and an inside pocket, this zip-closure tote is road-ready.

Finished tote size: approximately 15" x 15" x 3½" (excluding straps)

SUPPLIES

- ¾ yard of 54"- to 60"-wide wool plaid for tote exterior
- 5" x 17" rectangle of faux leather for tote bottom
- ¾ yard of 60"-wide lightweight Cordura nylon for lining
- 1¼ yards of 36"-wide woven, sew-in interfacing
- 1 yard of stiff fusible interfacing (such as fast2fuse)
- ½ yard of lightweight fusible knit interfacing
- 1 yard of ⅜"-wide iron-on adhesive such as HeatnBond
- One 26"-long separating or double-pull zipper
- Matching all-purpose thread
- 1 set of 23"-long leather handles
- 4 metal handbag feet
- Marking pencil
- Teflon press cloth
- Rotary cutter and mat (optional)

Sources

Floriani provided the Heat N' Stitch, which is distributed by RNK Distributing (www.rnkdistributing.com).

Therm O Web (www.thermoweb.com) provided the HeatnBond iron-on adhesive.

CUTTING

From the wool plaid, cut two 16" x 19½" rectangles for the tote front and back, one 8" x 13" rectangle on the bias for the inside pocket, two 4" x 16" rectangles on the bias for the zipper facings, and one 3" x 20" rectangle on the bias for the handle tabs.

From the faux leather, cut one 4½" x 16" rectangle for the tote bottom.

From the nylon, cut one 4½" x 16" rectangle for the tote bottom and two 16" x 19½" rectangles for the tote front and back.

From the sew-in interfacing, cut one 4½" x 16" rectangle for the tote bottom and two 16½" x 19½" rectangles for the tote front and back.

From the craft interfacing, cut one 3½" x 15" rectangle for the tote bottom and two 15" squares for the tote front and back.

From the fusible interfacing, cut one 8" x 13" rectangle and three 1" x 6" strips for the inside pocket, two 4" x 16" rectangles for the zipper facings, and one 3" x 20" rectangle for the handle tabs.

CONSTRUCTING THE BAG PIECES

Sew with right sides together and a ½" seam allowance unless otherwise noted.

Tote Body, Feet & Handles

1. Baste the sew-in interfacing to the wrong side of the wool tote body pieces and the faux leather bottom piece, stitching ⅜" from the raw edges. Trim the interfacing close to the stitching.

2. Position each craft interfacing square on the wool tote body pieces wrong side, centering them between the upper and lower stitching lines and side seams; fuse.

3. Fuse the knit interfacing to the wrong side of the bias plaid zipper facings, pocket and handle tab, taking care to maintain each piece's original shape.

4. On the wrong side of the faux leather tote bottom piece, center the 3½" x 15" craft interfacing rectangle and fuse following the manufacturer's instructions.

5. Mark the feet placement measuring 1½" in from each side at the corners (fig. A). Align the feet prongs with the marks, making two small clips through all layers. Insert the feet and spread the prongs on the wrong side to secure.

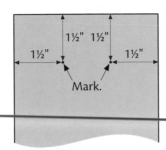

Fig. A
Mark feet placement.

6. Fold the bias handle tab in half lengthwise. Pin and stitch the long edge using a ⅜" seam allowance. Press the seam open and turn right side out. Center the seam to the back and press. Cut the tab into four 5" lengths.

7. Turn the tabs under ½" at each end and press. Topstitch ¼" from the fold and trim close to the stitching.

8. With the seam side up, pin one folded edge of each tab 3¼" from the tote body 19½" upper edge and 5½" from one side. Edgestitch, forming a 1" square on the tab end (fig. B). Repeat for the remaining handle tabs.

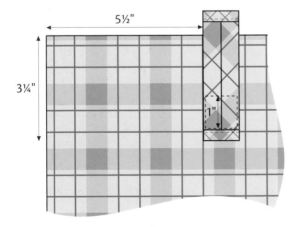

Fig. B
Pin tab to tote; edgestitch.
Repeat with remaining tabs.

9. On the tote bottom wrong side, make a dot in each corner ½" from each edge.

10. Center the tote bottom on one tote body lower edge, 1¾" from each side edge; pin. Stitch the long edge between the marks (fig. C). Press the seam open.

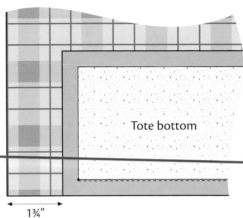

Fig. C
Center tote bottom; pin and stitch.

11. On the tote body only, clip the seam allowance to the marks. Repeat to join the remaining side to the bottom. Pin the tote sides together and stitch. Press the seams open.

12. Center the tote-body side seam on the short ends of the tote bottom. Pin in place and stitch from clip to clip (fig. D). Press the seams open.

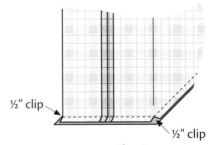

Fig. D
Center side seam on
tote bottom short end; stitch.

FEET FINESSE

To enhance a bag or tote's look and durability, consider adding metal feet. Found in most notions departments, the feet are not only stylish but also practical—protecting the bag's bottom when resting on a soiled surface.

To apply the feet, measure and mark the placement 1" inside the finished seam for a tote the size of the project shown. If making a smaller bag, scale down the measurement proportionately and use smaller feet. Use the prongs of the feet and either make an impression by pressing them into the fabric, or dust the prong tips with tailor's chalk. Snip the marked points on the fabric and insert the prongs. Once inserted, spread the prongs for a firm fit and smooth the panel to eliminate wrinkles.

Metal feet raise the tote so it won't get as dirty when set on a soiled surface.

Pocket, Lining, Facings & Zipper

1. With right sides together, fold the 8" x 13" plaid rectangle in half widthwise. Stitch around all three sides, leaving a 2" opening along the long edge. Trim the seam allowances to ¼" and clip across the corners. Turn the pocket right side out, and turn in the opening's seam allowances; press.

2. Place two 1" x 6" fusible interfacing strips vertically on the wrong side of the tote front lining, 5¾" from each side and 5¼" from the upper edge. Place the remaining strip horizontally between the two vertical strips, 4¾" from the lower edge (fig. E); fuse in place.

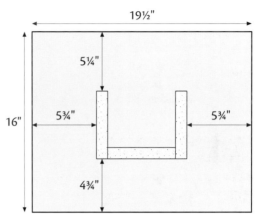

Fig. E
Fuse interfacing strips to lining wrong side.

3. Center the pocket on the right side of the front lining 5" from the upper edge and 6¼" from the sides with the edges overlapping the interfacing strips on the wrong side. Edgestitch the pocket sides and lower edges, and then topstitch ¼" from the edgestitching.

4. Sew the lining following the same instructions as for the tote body and bottom, leaving a 10" opening in one of the lining side seams for turning.

5. Fold each zipper facing in half lengthwise. Stitch across each short end. Clip across the corners and trim the seam allowance to ¼". Turn right side out and press flat.

6. With the zipper right side up, place a 15" length of iron-on adhesive on each zipper tape 5⅜" from each end. Fuse following the manufacturer's instructions.

7. Place a facing folded edge right side up on each side of the zipper; adhere in place.

8. Topstitch the facing to the zipper ⅛" and again ⅜" from the folded edge.

Extended zippers allow the tote to open fully when unzipped.

9. Center and pin the zipper facing to the tote upper edges. Stitch, and then press the seams open.

FINISHING

1. With the handle right side up, slip one handle end onto a tab. Fold the tab down, enclosing the handle and matching the ends. Edgestitch along the previous stitching line and 1½" above (fig. F). Repeat to attach the opposite end and the remaining handle.

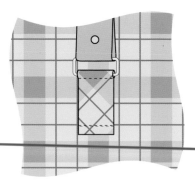

Fig. F
Fold tab through handle;
match ends and edgestitch.

2. With right sides together, slip the tote inside the lining. Pin the upper edges together, aligning the side seams. Stitch, and then trim the seam allowance to ¼". Press the seam toward the lining.

3. Gently pull the tote through the hole in the lining. Pin the lining edges together and edgestitch the opening closed. Tuck the lining into the tote, and press the upper edge.

4. Hand stitch along the upper and lower side seams, catching the lining to secure.

TRAVELING LIGHT

Designed by Kate Van Fleet

THIS LITTLE BAG IS JUST THE RIGHT SIZE to fit an airport-compliant plastic bag filled with regulation toiletries. Simple appliqué and satin stitching give your bag a personal touch.

Finished bag size: approximately 7" x 10"

SUPPLIES

- Two 8½" x 11" rectangles each of solid fabric, coordinating print fabric, fusible interfacing and fusible fleece
- Scraps of coordinating print fabric for appliqué(s)
- Paper-backed fusible web
- 9"-long coordinating zipper
- Thread: matching all-purpose, coordinating embroidery

CUTTING

From the solid fabric, coordinating fabric, fusible fleece and interfacing, cut two pouches each using the pattern on page 93 (enlarge 125%).

APPLIQUÉING THE BAG

1. Fuse interfacing to each fabric wrong side. Fuse the fleece to each lining wrong side.

2. Adhere the fusible web to the coordinating fabric wrong side following the manufacturer's instructions. Leave the paper backing intact. Draw a mirror image of a letter or draw several letters to create a monogram on the paper backing. Cut out the letter appliqué(s) following the drawn lines. Remove the paper backing.

3. Audition the appliqué(s) on one solid fabric pouch right side. When satisfied with the placement, fuse the appliqué(s) in place.

4. Satin stitch around the appliqué, using coordinating embroidery thread.

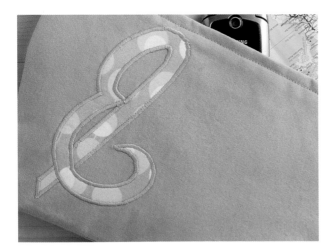

CONSTRUCTING THE BAG

Sew with right sides together and a ¼" seam allowance unless otherwise noted.

1. Fold the appliquéd pouch piece upper edge ½" toward the wrong side; press. Fold the remaining solid and coordinating pouch piece upper edges ½" toward the wrong side; press.

2. Baste the zipper in place along each solid fabric upper fold, following the zipper manufacturer's instructions.

3. Stitch the zipper. Remove the basting thread; open the zipper. Stitch the solid pouch pieces together along the side and lower edges.

4. Trim the corners and turn the bag right side out through the zipper.

5. Stitch the lining fabric pouch pieces together along the side and lower edges. The fusible fleece upper edge will be between the lining upper fold.

6. Insert the lining into the outer pouch with wrong sides facing and upper edges aligned.

7. Hand stitch the lining upper edge in place to conceal the zipper tape raw edge.

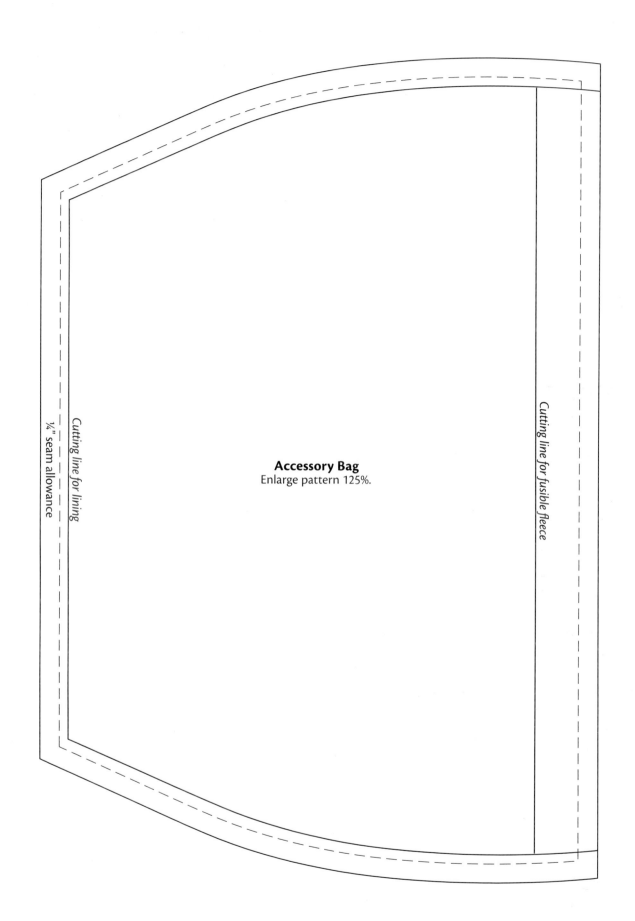

Accessory Bag
Enlarge pattern 125%.

Cutting line for fusible fleece

Cutting line for lining

¼" seam allowance

WATER-BOTTLE SLING

Designed by Ellen March

KEEP YOUR WATER BOTTLE WITH YOU AT ALL TIMES with this handy sling. You'll stay refreshed and hydrated all day long.

Finished size: 4¼" x 11½" (excluding strap)

SUPPLIES

Yardages are based on 54"-wide fabric.

- ⅓ yard of brown waterproof fabric (such as Denier Packcloth) for sling exterior and lining
- ⅓ yard of blue waterproof fabric for pocket and strap
- Two ¾" D-rings
- ½" metal leash clip
- ¾" buckle slide
- Matching all-purpose thread

CUTTING

From the brown fabric, cut two 9½" x 12½" rectangles for the sling body and lining, three 1½" x 2½" rectangles for the strap tabs and two 7"-diameter circles for the sling bottom.

From the blue fabric, cut one 9½" x 12½" rectangle for the pocket and one 3" x 50" rectangle for the strap.

CONSTRUCTING THE SLING

Sew with right sides together and a ½" seam allowance unless otherwise noted.

1. With wrong sides together, fold the blue rectangle in half lengthwise. Stitch close to the fold. Align the blue rectangle long raw edge with one brown rectangle long raw edge; stitch the blue rectangle to the brown rectangle, leaving the upper folded edge free. Stitch down the pocket center through all layers and perpendicular to the fold to create two pockets (fig. A).

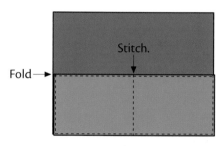

Fig. A

2. With right sides together, fold the brown rectangles in half lengthwise, and then stitch the long raw edges. Turn the tubes right sides out. Fold the long edges of the blue strap rectangle so they meet in the center of the strip, wrong sides together; press, using a press cloth. Fold the strip in half lengthwise, enclosing the raw edges. Edgestitch around the perimeter of the strap and each tab. Fold each tab in half widthwise and press, using a press cloth.

3. Thread one strap end through a D-ring. Turn under the raw edge, and then stitch close to the fold to encase the D-ring. Thread the other strap end through the buckle slide, through the remaining D-ring, and then through the middle buckle slide slot (fig. B). Fold under the raw end and stitch close to the fold.

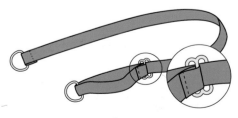

Fig. B

4. Thread a tab through each D-ring. Stitch as close to the D-ring as the presser foot allows (fig. C).

Fig. C

5. Thread the remaining tab through the leash clip, and then stitch as close to the clip as the presser foot allows.

6. Position the leash clip tab below the pocket center stitching with the tab stitching aligned with the fabric lower edge; pin, and then stitch in place. Position the D-ring tabs equidistant from each other along the brown rectangle upper edge. Align the tab stitching with the fabric raw edge; pin, and then stitch in place.

7. Fold the brown rectangle (with pocket) in half widthwise. Stitch the short raw edges with a ¼" seam allowance. Stitch one circle to the tube lower edge. Clip the curves. Turn the tube right side out. Stitch the remaining rectangle short raw edges, leaving a 3" opening for turning. Stitch the remaining circle to the tube lower edge as previously directed.

8. Right sides together, push one tube inside the other and stitch the upper edges. Make sure the strap doesn't get caught in the stitching. Turn the tube right side out through the opening. Hand stitch the opening closed. Push the lining tube inside the outer tube and finger-press the upper edge.

9. Insert a water bottle, attach keys to the leash clip, and use the pockets for a granola bar and I.D. card. Have a good workout!

tip

Experiment with fabrics you have on hand—use quilting cottons and treat them with waterproofing spray prior to construction. Or use neoprene or coated canvas for a different look.

ABOUT THE CONTRIBUTORS

Pamela K. Archer lives, sews and teaches in the greater Portland, OR area. A longtime fiber fanatic, Pam shares her love of sewing through classes and freelance writing for several sewing publications. She's the author of *Fast, Fun and Easy Fabric Bags* and *Fast, Fun and Easy Home Accents*.

Beth Bradley has always been fascinated by fashion. She learned to sew in high school and went on to earn a degree in Apparel Design and Production. Beth is currently the Associate Editor of *Sew News* magazine.

Diane Giancola is a well-known educator specializing in sewing notions and fabric dyeing. She has appeared on many TV shows, including *America Quilts Creatively* and *Sewing with Nancy*. Diane also has experience in the home-sewing industry as Education Manager for a large thread manufacturer and as Director of Communications for a sewing notions company.

Linda Turner Griepentrog is the owner of G Wiz Creative Services, specializing in writing and designing for the sewing, embroidery, quilting and crafting industries. She's the author of four books: *Machine Embroidery Wild & Wacky*, *Embroidery Machine Essentials—Quilting Techniques*, *Print Your Own Fabric* and *Needle Felting by Hand or Machine*.

Linda Lee is the owner of The Sewing Workshop Pattern Collection, a group of patterns for distinctive garments using innovative sewing techniques. A licensed interior designer and member of ASID since 1974, Linda has written 13 books. Visit www.sewingworkshop.com for more information.

Ellen March has sewing in her blood. At 16, she starred in the educational film *Picking Your Pattern, Fabric and Notions*, and has since appeared on DIY's *Uncommon Threads* and on PBS's *MacPhee Workshop*. Ellen is currently the editor of *Sew News*, *Sew It All* and *Creative Machine Embroidery* magazines.

Kaari Meng and her husband, Juan Carlos, own French General, a small vintage craft shop in Hollywood. Filled with beautiful crafting materials, the store offers inspiration and creativity for a "textured" life. French General's book, *Home Sewn*, is a guide to simple projects inspired by the florals and ticking stripes of the 1800s-era South of France.

Shannon Dennis is currently an independent author and professed omni-crafter living in Cleveland, OH. She's the founder of Nina (www.theninaline.com) and writes for a number of print and online publications.

Pauline Richards lives in Salt Lake City. She enjoys creative sewing and embellishing and publishes *Total Embellishment Newsletter*. View more of Pauline's creations at www.tennews.homestead.com.

Nancy Shriber is a textile artist and designs under the Contemporary Sashiko label. She enjoys sharing her passion for making beautiful things through retreats and workshops. Visit www.contemporarysashiko.com for more information.

Lisa Shepard Stewart is an author and designer specializing in African fabrics for sewing, decorating and quilting. Her third book, *African Accents ON THE GO! Designing Accessories with Cultural Style*, features 22 original handbag, tote and take-along projects to sew. Visit www.culturedexpressions.com.

Kate Van Fleet lives in Denver. An experienced garment sewer, she's made everything from prom gowns to business suits. She's the former owner of Kreations by Kate, a business supplying custom handmade pillows to nine stores in five states.

Joan Vardanega learned to sew from her favorite teacher, her mother. When she's not traveling to a sewing show, Joan loves to teach her daughter, son and a beginning 4-H sewing group.